THE LIQU

The Liquid Enterprise *is the first work to take an unflinching look at the unenviable job of transformation leadership, through the eyes of the leader. Taking us far beyond the usual digital platitudes, Michael Bayler once again challenges his readers to discard everything they know, in exchange for an entirely fresh view of strategy that, finally, is fit for today's and tomorrow's purpose.*

Richard Mosley, Global Vice President of Strategy, Universum, author of Employer Brand Management

Everyone's talking about change and disruption, but no one seems to have the instructions. Until now. The Liquid Enterprise *explains exactly what we've all been worrying about, why that is, and how to rethink business strategy for a future that demands we constantly transform – or die.*

Brian Wong, Founder and CEO, Kiip

The Liquid Enterprise *squares up to a Gordian Knot that is the single most important problem facing big businesses today – how to convert the chronic uncertainty that undermines our confidence in the future into our most powerful strategic weapon. Michael Bayler slices through that knot with simplicity, brevity and wit.*

Tony Ageh, OBE, BBC Controller

We need a completely new set of rules to navigate such a turbulent world. This easily digested book shows the way. Read, ponder and decide for yourself just how much of our classical management theory is still relevant.

Dr William Webb, CEO Weightless SIG, President of the Institution of Engineering and Technology, 2014–2015

Michael Bayler is a renowned business thinker, speaker, consultant and leadership mentor, inspiring strategic transformation across enterprise, technology and marketing.

He has ignited change programmes for many of the world's largest brands. His clients have included Coca-Cola, the BBC, Unilever, Diageo, Telefonica, Egg, FremantleMedia, PayPal, Bacardi Global Brands, Warner Bros., BSkyB, SABMiller, British Telecom, Sony Music, Robbie Williams and Simon Cowell.

Michael is the co-author of *Promiscuous Customers: Invisible Brands – Delivering Value in Digital Markets* (Capstone, Oxford, 2002).

THE LIQUID ENTERPRISE

*How The Network is transforming value,
the implications for business, and
what leadership needs to do about it*

Michael Bayler

infinite ideas

The paradox of mechanization is that although it is itself the cause of maximal growth and change, the principle of mechanization excludes the very possibility of growth or the understanding of change.

Marshall McLuhan

———————————

A philosophical question has the form: 'I don't know my way about'.

Ludwig Wittgenstein

Contents

Thanks   ix

Foreword   x

Introduction   1

1. The certainty trap   10

2. The efficiency trap   21

3. The experience trap   32

4. The innovation trap   48

5. Network disruption   55

6. Value disruption   64

7. Liquid objects   73

8. Liquid living   86

9.   Liquid customers   103

10. Liquid brands   115

11. Liquid enterprise   126

12. Liquid leadership   142

13. Thirteen things   155

Thanks

Many generous individuals – friends, colleagues and clients – have helped me to make this book a reality. Thanks in particular to David Stoughton, Tom Daly, Kate Harrison, Donald Shields, Jarle Holm, Judie Lannon, Jonathan Beardsworth, and Dr Michael Squirrell.

Thanks to the team at Infinite Ideas, whose support is priceless.

And of course, thanks to my family, with my love.

Foreword

The Liquid Enterprise is, I believe, the first accessible management book to link the profound challenges facing modern incumbent businesses with the dynamics of the global networks on which they now trade.

Its publication could not be more timely.

The author discovers, explores and explains a single fact – that the evidence we aim to use to justify our business decisions is now accumulating so quickly that we are swamped under it rather than being able to extract clarity from it.

Certainty based on evidence, which has for so long been such a robust and valid touchstone for enterprise leadership and management, has become impossible, and if we continue to pursue it, it turns into a serious threat, in a context where the combined speed and complexity of data make effective aggregation, interpretation, action and reaction impossible.

That context has undeniably arrived, and as Michael Bayler unfolds his simple, logical, and revolutionary tale, we come to see that the very uncertainty that prevents us making rapid decisions can itself be shifted, to form a persuasive premise for new ways of thinking about business, new forms of competitive advantage, and, correspondingly, a new philosophy and shape demanded of the enterprises who stand to weather the storm.

I can speak to the issue directly, from my own professional experience.

When we founded Ofcom, the UK's communications regulator, a pertinent innovation was introduced early on, called 'evidence-based regulation'. It was at the time a concept few could disagree with – the opposite, whatever that might be, does not sound palatable.

But – and this applies in particular in the case of a regulator whose entire remit covers the evolution and dynamics of networks – it very soon emerged that basing strategic decisions on evidence can no longer provide adequate assurance.

By the time there is sufficient proof that a policy or strategy could be advantageous, it is already out of date.

We live and trade in a world of big data, where the

volumes of information generated are so great we can no longer hope to analyse them before exponentially more arrives. This state of affairs is guaranteed to become more chaotic. The Internet of Things is already injecting more swathes of data into our world, and will surely come to overturn familiar business models and the globally recognized brands that serve them.

And yet we are still rigorously trained and fully expected to assess the evidence before making decisions.

In the business world, new companies like Uber, Airbnb and of course Amazon, Google and Facebook, appear, grow and disrupt whole sectors in just a few years, while traditional powerhouses visibly struggle to get to grips with an environment they feel ill-equipped to address.

As we look at these huge poster children and marvel at the speed with which they have come to dominate their spaces, we rarely ask ourselves 'what evidence did they use to justify their strategies?' Where was the proof that a taxi app would create a revolution in transport, or indeed that a better search engine would become massively profitable?

To the contrary, and famously in the case of Apple's iPod, most of these companies became successful despite respectable research clearly suggesting their approach would fail.

Culturally, we have felt sure that clear and incisive strategic direction is a mark of strong leadership: our case studies are resplendent with examples of this. Our management philosophy comes from history, from MBA courses. Like generals from another age, we assume that this battle should be fought the same way as the last.

But a look around us makes it clear these 'truths' are no longer valid. *The Liquid Enterprise* helps us understand first of all why, and then how we need to change, in order to catch up with the world. We must learn to 'tap into the flow' rather than continuing to try to collect it behind a dam.

There will from here be very few reliable certainties. Leaders who experiment, hedge bets, change direction and admit mistakes are more likely to succeed than those who insist on holding fast to their one big bet. Far, however, from being a tip sheet for gambling with the enterprise, readers should approach this book as conclusively summarizing both a compelling need, and a revolutionary rationale, for the most important disruption of all: a fresh, modern and fit for purpose way of doing strategy.

We need a completely new set of rules to navigate such a turbulent world. This easily digested book shows the way. Read, ponder and decide for yourself just how much of our classical management theory is still relevant.

Dr William Webb,
CEO, Weightless SIG, President of The Institution
of Engineering and Technology, 2014–2015

Introduction

What to think?

You will already have noted, I expect with relief, that this is not a large book.

Nobody who is responsible for leading a business of any size, or indeed for advising leadership, hungers greatly for yet more content.

We are looking for answers, for understanding, and above all for the ability to make confident, clear decisions, based on accessible accounts of what is happening now, what it means for the near future, and what we should do about it in order to defend and grow the enterprise.

This has, it's fair to say, never been more difficult.

Uncertainty about the dynamics of whatever market we may find ourselves in, the boundaries between this and other markets, from which it seems disruptive competition can emerge at any time, the needs and wants of customers, and perhaps above all, the role and impacts of technologies that offer, in equal measure, threats to the way we think about value, and opportunities to define and capture it in entirely new ways, defines the mood in businesses everywhere.

The Liquid Enterprise aims to begin the urgent process of changing the way we think about these subjects, and in particular the way strategy itself needs now to fundamentally change, in order to usefully perform its role of interpreting the cultural and commercial context, to enable us to bring to market, and profitably exploit, compelling and competitive products and services.

It's worth immediately making a robust distinction between strategy, planning and execution.

I believe, very simply, that strategy is about how we think about what we need to think, planning is how we think about what we need to do, and in turn, execution, or delivery, is about how we do what we need to do.

In this sense, *The Liquid Enterprise* is entirely a book about strategy.

There is, in the flood of published business books, no shortage of generally good advice about what we can call 'the how'. And yet leadership and its advisors find themselves in a genuine quandary about the context within which decisions about why things are the way they are now, and therefore what to do, are made.

Before we turn, with the necessary rationales in place, to getting on with doing what needs to be done, we urgently need to grasp 'the why' and 'the what'.

Crisis and opportunity

Some fifteen years ago, I began with my old friend and invaluable collaborator David Stoughton a project that emerged in early 2002 as the book *Promiscuous Customers: Invisible Brands – Delivering Value in Digital Markets*. At the time, the explosive promise of the Internet had faltered and thrown us into what was called 'the dotcom crash'.

There's no need to go over that well-covered ground again here, but with an eye to our current position, and especially the sharp contrast between the combination of rapid cultural change and profound commercial uncertainty that featured at the time, and that is now with us once again, the parallels are striking.

At that time, unlike today, few of the key pieces were as yet on the board. There were no smartphones, no Wi-Fi, broadband was embryonic, and the unforgettable squeal of the dial-up modem was everywhere.

As a result, the process of writing *Promiscuous Customers* was not dissimilar to doing a large load of laundry in public.

In order to produce a work that was fit for purpose, we were obliged to lay out a depth and range of theoretical thinking that, to say the least, taxed both writers and readers heavily. This was not a book for the beach.

However, and gratifyingly, given the size of the rock we had to push up that hill – not to mention our strong desire to never have to repeat this gruelling process – the book successfully articulated many of the key dynamics of the still-emerging forms of digital value that we take for granted today.

It also managed, with luck as much as insight, to anticipate some of today's foundational elements, such as the Internet of Things, information-enabled customer service as a core enterprise focus, and, more recently, a determined push back by customers wielding unprecedented power over media, against the over-aggressive targeting and tracking of advertising by publishers and brands.

There were, we also discovered, a number of strategic misconceptions that were compromising enterprise strategy. Chief among these was the natural assumption that information is, in and of itself, an entirely good thing for business.

Unfettered information, it turns out, can not only erode enterprise value, but also unpick and pull apart traditionally secure and predictable value chains, to expose entire industry sectors, along with a well-documented list of previously powerful incumbents, to the prospect of trying to trade in what have become chaotic, and often hostile, ecosystems.

This dynamic has since played out at a global scale, as the universal flow of communication across networks of all kinds, more recently extending to the physical, creates a constantly accelerating and more complex tsunami of bewildering disruption.

It has evolved, in fact, into what we can call The Network.

The Network both forms and informs the context in which enterprises must learn to act and react with a speed, intelligence and flexibility that, even looking back just a decade, feel utterly unfamiliar.

Meeting the new challenges

We are now, painfully and slowly, emerging from the worst global financial crisis in close to a century.

Closely mirroring the mood of fifteen years ago, but with the stakes sharply raised by the increasingly disruptive force of The Network, we find ourselves at another crossroads.

On one hand, giant competitors such as Uber and Airbnb are emerging, leveraging market forces that, despite their disruptive presence and eye-watering growth and valuations, we have yet to come to grips with.

On the other, incumbent businesses, owners of the most powerful brands in the world, are suddenly on the back foot, with little or no confident vision of a viable way forward.

Making sense of the market – any market – equipped only with the traditional tools of business strategy, is our most urgent challenge.

This unenviable position demands nothing short of a radical reframing of the environment, an uncompromising look at the unfamiliar dynamics of unrelenting change, and above all, a transformative philosophy that will equip us to shape and constantly reshape the enterprise in ways that reflect, rather than resist, the new dynamics of value and risk that define business on The Network.

While, unlike fifteen years ago, many of the pieces may now be on the board, the rules of the new game of business on The Network remain stubbornly resistant to understanding.

This is, from here on, an environment primarily defined by uncertainty.

Making a start

The Liquid Enterprise will not provide us with everything we need to move forward. It is, as pointed out earlier, a 'why' and 'what' book.

The 'how' will be addressed in future publications that will focus initially on methodology, and subsequently on practical application.

Before we are able to make even the broadest of strategic decisions about, for example, where to invest, how to operationalize, and the corresponding allocation of resources, we need to challenge and replace many of the beliefs, models and behaviours that may have served us well until recently, and prepare ourselves to think in a very different way.

As I also mentioned above, I believe that brevity is the *sine qua non* of a good and useful business book, as well as being a consequence of a fully considered argument.

While this book is, necessarily, by no means an easy read, I've tried to make it as logical and accessible as the complex and still-emerging territory allows.

You will find no case studies, charts or statistics in *The Liquid Enterprise*. There is no shortage of these available elsewhere, and, to be frank, in the absence of a fresh and comprehensive account of the environment, which is the intent here, they don't seem to have helped us a great deal to date. Evidence without hypothesis is worthless.

This is, above all, a story: as far as possible, a simple narrative framing of how we got here, what it means, and how we need to think about moving forward.

While offering a fresh and, I hope in the end, pragmatic view of how we need to think about strategy from now, this book is only the beginning of an important and wide-ranging conversation.

As well as, where you see fit, making your own notes, I invite to you send me thoughts and further questions by email to michael@bayler.com. The resulting discussions will be published and regularly updated on my blog, *The Strategy Review*.

The certainty trap

The new challenge of uncertainty · decision quality
in turbulence · early responses to disruption ·
technology as a threat · embracing turbulence ·
from evidence to confidence.

Not knowing

Arguably the core role of enterprise leadership is to assess, decide and commit to degrees of certainty.

This has never been more challenging, and it will
become far more so, far more quickly than we'd like, due
to radical and irreversible changes in the dynamics of
business.

This problem is, all the evidence suggests, here to stay.

As more data – information and communication – floods
The Network, both change and complexity will continue to
accelerate. The effect of this brutal pincer movement is to

make confident decision quality, in the familiar forms we have known it, impossible.

Change is no longer in any sense linear, which makes even approximated estimates, let alone predictions, too variable for comfort.

We could say that the word change itself, presuming as it does some sort of constant, a 'fixed location where we can stand', 'a place where we're going to or coming from', is becoming redundant.

The notion of perpetual, pervasive turbulence better captures the current and future context.

As the rate and volume of data increases alongside this turbulence, our ability to make sense of it, to gather and apply it usefully to create and validate the hypotheses we need, in order to invest in and harvest enterprise value, is consistently and progressively diluted.

For data of any kind to inform decision-making, it needs, at least to a workable degree, to be susceptible to interpretation. We must be able to distinguish and extract meaningful signal from noise.

To usefully do so today and tomorrow, we would be effectively required to create and integrate new categories of information – fields, in database terms – at more or less the same speed at which all this new data is flooding in.

And in order to make those kinds of selections, we would be in turn required to make more or less real time decisions as to which kinds of information matter, which changes – today, as opposed to yesterday or 10 minutes ago – are now important.

This deafening cacophony of bits is, as we battle to contain and to make sense of it, no longer an asset. It's an indefatigable enemy of confident business strategy, of planning, and of execution.

We could liken this leadership challenge to playing an extended game of chess, one where the pieces on the board move around between moves, and both opponents and allies come and go without warning.

Worse, the very rules of the game change, sometimes subtly, sometimes destructively, without warning.

We reach a point, if we follow this metaphor a step further, where the game becomes unplayable. It no longer has recognisable, manageable rules. We're no longer playing chess at all.

This unfolding, chronic condition informs the prevailing sense of confusion amongst the leadership of incumbent enterprises. It's now officially hard to convincingly lead anything, or anyone, anywhere.

Confusion is an understandable and appropriate response to the new dynamics of business. Now is not the time for bullish statements of false clarity, nor for resting on past laurels; least of all, for toughing it out.

Any form of denial – which we could have perhaps in the past got away with, if only because the market moved so relatively slowly, competition was more or less predictable, and customer expectations were correspondingly low – is no longer helpful.

Letting go of old friends

Many established firms are, again understandably in this context, seeking reliable sources of reassurance: a return, even temporarily, to an acceptable form of certainty, a base from which to credibly define what we must respond to, and what in turn our response should look like.

We will explore these further in the next chapters because, before we can move forward to accept and embrace the race against the turbulence and complexity that form the landscape of future leadership decision making, we must reluctantly let go of a previous, profound and powerful mind set, one that insists upon a solid base, a reliable and adequately fixed and shared worldview.

At the time of writing, a range of philosophies – and corresponding change projects – are framing the declared strategic responses of the majority of incumbent companies, and the sectors within which they trade.

The overall challenge is, most commonly, referred to as disruption. The new network giants we touched on in the introduction are the poster children for just how bad – and, on a good day, just how very good – our disruptive futures could be.

Among these responses, the digital transformation of the enterprise, and competition through optimized customer experience, both couched on a reassuringly rich and fertile, not to mention big, bed of valuable data, are the dominant themes.

Alongside these, we have a universal obsession with innovation, in recognition of our urgent need to change many different aspects of the ways in which we create value, faster than we ever have before.

All of these interim solutions have a current and ongoing validity, by the way, assuming that they are rapidly and sure-footedly executed.

But none of them will protect us from the gathering storm.

We must come to see them for what they are: in some cases, the concluding chapters of a previous narrative, in others, the opening, scene-setting ones for a next, radically different, story.

We must look beyond the digital horizon.

Overall, technology is the focus. And yet its role across both culture and commerce is, in terms of our concerns about uncertainty, somewhat schizophrenic.

On one hand, there is realistically no significant area of life or business that is not influenced, indeed determined, by technology. It is, in this sense, an entirely reliable constant.

On the other, technology continues to throw up a flood of inventions from all directions, each of whose potential impact often remains obscure, but each of which seems to demand our attention.

What does this mean? What does it mean for us? Is it marginal, something for later, or a central disruption, a hitherto unseen iceberg to our Titanic?

Technology is as much a consistent and implacable

driver of the problem, as it is a provider of magical solutions. And it's the former that we need to come to terms with.

For the engineer, and, for a little while perhaps, the marketer, technology is an eternal touchstone for what matters, for the construction and measurement of value.

For leadership, at best, it relentlessly drives and shakes up a chaotic context, one from which we must discover and extract a new way of thinking about value.

A new way, in fact, of doing business.

Embracing uncertainty

Recently, before delivering a keynote titled 'Objects In Mirror … What Comes After Digital?' to an audience largely made up of financial services technology leaders, I asked a tough question.

Which of us believes that the business we're in today will be, more or less, recognisable in five years?

No one, out of about a hundred, raised their hand.

How about three years? Again, no hands.

Taking into account the state of play in that particular industry – notoriously in need of change, infamously slow to do so, and painfully aware of the massed bandits of disruptive, investor-friendly fintechs gathering on the hills above – its leadership still recognize that they have no more than between three and five years in which to radically change the shape of both the sector and the incumbent enterprises that form it.

This is, by the way, an optimistic timeframe for any substantial enterprise transformation to take root. Pulling no punches, by the time today's vision of the future shape of any sector is anywhere near realized, it's already in danger of being redundant.

There is, we learn, no place to make a solid stand. At least the way we once did.

But there is both good news, and a tangible way forward.

As we come to see our disruptions, our transformations and our innovations for what they are, at least in their current temporary abode – the remaining vestiges of a previous certainty that we have relied upon – we are freed to consider new, logical and eventually exciting and reassuring ways of thinking about enterprise survival and manageable growth.

As soon as we accept uncertainty, a fresh basis for competitive advantage emerges.

On this temporarily level playing field, the enterprise that actively engages with uncertainty, learns to work with it, to flex, to scale and to pivot in some sort of step with its dance, is given the opportunity to acquire new skills, and to build an entirely new set of core capabilities.

The most important among these will be a central, progressive and enterprise-wide ability to grasp, to manage – and to take full competitive advantage of – that same profound uncertainty that is the cause of our current bewilderment.

From evidence to confidence

To achieve this, one fundamental shift in the way those in leadership think needs to occur.

We have – and the digital revolution's torrent of available data has done much to reinforce and further embed this – come to rely on quantity and quality of information to both inform and validate our decision quality.

The management, we could say, of evidence, has become an accepted core capability of modern business.

But when, as I hope we're now seeing, the very context within which the data resides, and on which it depends for any sort of actionable meaning, is in a state of increasing flux – always tending towards chaos, we could say – evidence, which has always been relative to its context, becomes unreliable.

It becomes far too transient for comfort.

Our response? We start to apply a new and unfamiliar discipline. We learn to manage – to decide and act upon – degrees of relative confidence.

When every firm, as they soon enough will, has access to more or less the same heaving pools of data, the new competitive advantage, one that should, with focus and good fortune, prove in itself to be sustainable, is built on the active and deliberate management of confidence.

This will begin life as an uncomfortable and unfamiliar cultural challenge for leadership.

It will then start to make sense as a philosophy. From here it will evolve to form the heart of a new strategic methodology, one whose entire purpose and effect is the conversion of chronic uncertainty into fresh value and growth for the enterprise.

That momentarily calming vision notwithstanding, we remain for now in the foothills of our journey over the digital horizon.

We need to put our current endeavours into a more workable context, and to do so, we need to revisit and directly question a number of very basic, soon to become problematic, assumptions.

Chapter summary

- Business is, from here, done in a context of chronic turbulence;
- Certainty is no longer a reliable base for leadership decision quality;
- Digital transformation, customer experience and innovation programmes are interim, tactical solutions;
- Technology is both a consistent foundation for business and a source of strategic threat;
- Uncertainty is the new source of competitive advantage;
- The calculated management of degrees of confidence is the new core enterprise capability.

The efficiency trap

2

How technology frames and traps strategy • frozen
in the past • the what, the why and the how •
digital efficiency as a block to growth.

A hidden fault line

There is a very real sense in which every technology – no matter how fresh or ground breaking it may be in terms of the present and near future – is already a legacy technology.

We tend, entirely understandably, to believe that because a large degree of the chronically disruptive cultural and commercial context we face is clearly both propelled and defined by technology, and because our interpretation of the increasing turbulence that new offerings introduce, both regularly and unpredictably, into the environment, is framed in these terms, that technology itself will in turn hold the answers we seek.

Our strategic decisioning becomes, apparently quite naturally, framed and determined by reactions, followed by commitments, to what seem to be appropriate configurations of previous, past and anticipated technological innovations.

This, in many senses, and again assuming that such projects are more or less successful, is not in itself wrong.

But it's not enough.

As we'll come to see, this elemental world view represents a mental trap that, left unchallenged, focuses our thinking and our investments exclusively on finding and implementing technologies that, in the short term, respond to those transient priorities that we need to constantly challenge, understand and move beyond.

Technology, it's easy to forget, can only ever do precisely what it's told to do. No matter how powerful, sophisticated, analytical, responsive or predictive its behaviour is now – or how much more so it becomes – hidden behind every one of its extraordinary performances is … a calculator.

What comes out, inevitably, faithfully, and utterly without exception, reflects, like a mirror, what went in.

We are, and will remain, the trainers and instructors of our technology. If we fail to bear this in mind at every step, we fall victim to a way of thinking that is dangerously close to magical. The implications, as the future accelerates into the present, and the present slips rapidly into the past, are central to our discussion and demand careful consideration.

In our hunt for certainty of decisioning on behalf of the enterprise, we naturally build the systems that not only insist upon – or at least aspire to – this certainty, but that hard-wire our limited and temporary understanding of the current structure and dynamics of the market, the correspondingly optimal structure and dynamics of our businesses, and indeed the structure and dynamics of value itself, into the past.

As long as our systems remain mired in assumptions that the relative shapes of market, enterprise and value are now, and will remain, correct and consistent, we freeze in time our strategy, the very thing that now demands an unprecedented fluidity and flexibility.

Furthermore, this redundancy, in terms of the need to support the defence and growth of the enterprise going forward, deepens and becomes more threatening in direct proportion to the increase in turbulence that will, we know too well, itself only continue to grow.

As the pace of change increases, our technology – if left as it is and used in the way we have been using it – ages ever faster.

Looking past the technology

Such underlying assumptions regarding the central role and future value of technology, in the business context that we are coming to terms with here, are not merely hostile to our ability to defend and grow the enterprise. They reflect and impose on our journey a map of the world that is already historical, before we even set sail.

The one thing that our technology will never be able to do, as long as it's boxed in, as it were, by the intractable logic that we build into it, is unfreeze itself, tell us what's changed, how it's changing, and what we should do about it.

The turbulence of the environment will consistently throw increasing numbers and types of new, left-field questions at the enterprise and its systems.

Our technology, as long as it is exclusively guided by the historical strategic shapes we have built into it, is intrinsically unable to flex and twist to answer these questions, at least in a manner that provides the certainty of decisioning that is for now demanded of us.

This emerging conundrum, as I hope we are coming to see, is at the very core of the disquiet that leadership feels.

Our growing uncertainty is not based merely on not being quite sure what's going on – we have never, after all, had more information to work with – but on the far more disturbing realization that even the most advanced tools we may have to hand are never quite fit for purpose.

We have, we could say, an abundance of 'how' but not nearly enough 'why' or 'what'. If technology, in the end, can only process and provide certainty based upon the limited insight we are able to synthesize at any fixed point, and the context itself is chronically turbulent, then we can't sensibly expect it to fully equip us for the future.

It's the way we think about business, the way we do strategy itself, that needs to change.

Far from reacting with a Luddite rejection of the infinity of promise that new technology continues to hold out to us, we must, somehow, learn to live with and actively manage an eternal tension, between knowing and not knowing, committing and holding back, falling short and leaping ahead.

Reframing transformation

When we come to understand and accept the logic of this challenge – with the feeling that far from reaching calmer water, we are casting off on a new journey that makes our experience to date seem relatively benign – we are immediately presented with pressing questions regarding the eventual validity of what we have been calling 'digital business transformation programmes'.

This is a serious concern, in particular given the high levels of both expectation and expenditure that are currently vested in this approach to the future.

In the light of our thinking so far, is transformation, as we know it now, a major investment in precious resource and time that, far from preparing us for the disruptive future, to the contrary locks us into a comfortable but irrelevant set of redundant capabilities?

Both yes, and, to an extent, but only if we are brutally realistic, no.

As long as we imagine – and here is the danger of the magical thinking we touched on above – that such programmes in themselves offer a comprehensive, sustainable and predictable long-term platform for enterprise survival and growth, we are strategically putting the enterprise directly, and conclusively, in harm's way.

The word 'transformation' is a built-in part of the problem here. The current discourse almost invariably assumes that the overall effect will be to move the enterprise forward, to liberate it from too-slow processes, inadequate and out-of-date customer profiles, and clunky product and service development and delivery.

When looked at through the lens of the present moment, and on the basis that the market, the customer, and the overall environment itself will remain more or less stable, this is not unreasonable.

But our turbulent context no longer allows us the luxury, let alone the time, to believe that this will be the end of our race to certainty.

At its least productive, digital transformation simply makes us better, quicker, more responsive and, perhaps most appealingly in the absence of more compelling fresh propositions, far more cost-effective, at performing what were, at the time of specification, critical business functions. Getting better, we could say, at the things we needed to be really good at up to the recent past. But eventually at the expense of the capabilities we need to build for what comes next.

Some of these changes will remain valid for years, and some will hang on and, with the necessary tweaking and reintegration, eventually give way. The rest will likely already be a weight on the business by the time the work is finally delivered. Let's remember that the actual delivery time for even the most vanilla programme can easily stretch into several years.

Nevertheless, at its best, digital transformation delivers critical business efficiencies that provide the enterprise with a very necessary leanness, a certain amount of agility, and a temporary degree of improved customer service, along with the satisfaction of having introduced and integrated a range of fresh and exciting point innovations.

Programmes of efficiency

However we choose to approach transformation, and whatever the relative impact of the projects we may commit to, it can only fall short, in the absence of a radical shift in philosophy and expectation, in either protecting us from the increasing turbulence we face, or equipping us with the resilience, the flexibility and the competitive advantages we need to push forward with confidence.

But again, the news is not all bad.

When reframed as digital efficiency programmes, whose

intrinsic impact is understood from the start as being both temporary, and unlikely in isolation to strategically protect and prepare the enterprise for sustainable growth, these investments, alongside the time required for delivery, can be scaled accordingly and assessed under less demanding expectations and rational criteria.

Fixed and linear transformation programmes, we must be clear, can only typically deliver degrees of incremental improvement, results whose future implications will need rigorous revisiting and challenging – and yes, further investment – as the environment changes shape around them, and as the enterprise is driven forward to constantly reconsider and adjust its own shape.

They are not, in themselves, transformative to the conclusive extent that is hoped for.

Efficiency, the past has conclusively taught us, despite offering a temporary relief from pressures on margins, from the point of view of enterprise strategy, is an infamous block to growth.

Furthermore, a little-discussed but, in this context, critical lesson is that, contrary to common assumption, while efficiency may support agility, it does not in itself foster adaptability.

Quite the opposite: enterprise adaptability intrinsically demands immediate – or close to immediate – access to unused resources or capabilities. We will come back to this point later when we consider the central role of options in enabling adaptability on The Network.

If, in terms of focus and investment, we continue, having realized some early benefits, to depend upon systems and processes that serve only the efficiencies of the past, while ignoring the new and evolving advantages we need for the turbulent future, we are in fact excluding ourselves from building the very capabilities we most need in order to have a chance of survival and, from there, growth.

Without this abrupt, but very necessary shift in focus on the role and value of transformation as we currently know it, we are falling into The Efficiency Trap.

We are, we could say, fiddling, when we should be burning Rome.

Chapter summary

- An exclusive focus on technology creates fixed strategies that directly compromise future growth;

- Chronic turbulence demands a radically different strategic lens;
- Digital transformation, in itself, offers temporary efficiencies but not future competitive advantage;
- When reframed and invested in as 'rolling tactical improvements', it regains validity.

The experience trap

3

A brief history of customer experience • turbulence
disrupts the context • brand promise and delivery
converge in digital experience • experience as a
hygiene factor • the customer in control • the pizza
of value; the shift to service value • the invisible
brand.

The received wisdom

If there is one phrase that appears even more often than
transformation in the current vocabulary of enterprise
strategy, it is surely customer experience.

In my own work advising a lot of large brands, across
some two decades and a range of key industry sectors,
every company, in one form or another, has come to see
customer experience as at least a – very often *the* – key
driver of innovation and growth.

There is an entirely natural logic here. Who, after all, would not want their customer to have a good experience of the brand?

And yet, as with transformation, hidden underneath what seems like a powerful and reliable strategic touchstone, a valuable anchor of certainty in a turbulent market, are assumptions about both customer value and, as we'll see, meaning, that need substantial adjustment in order to avoid misplaced focus, expectation and, of course, investment.

How did we get here?

Broadly speaking, a customer's experience of any brand, before the digital revolution, was divided into two distinct areas of impact.

There was the promise – commonly some form of communication preceding purchase – and then, assuming a purchase, there was the ownership and usage of the product or service.

In other words, there was what the brand said about itself, and then the degree, in the context of actual ownership, to which the customer found the product more or less adequate in terms of what had been promised, and the individual experience of use.

It is essential to recognize that, under this model, 'the brand', as opposed to 'the product', was defined almost entirely by messaging distributed in advertisements, in promotions, and of course on packaging.

The brand was more or less completely owned and defined by its owner. The brand, in other words, drove the experience.

Behind this model lies the marketing imperative of customer mindshare. The role of advertising today remains largely to remind consumers that brands exist, and to reinforce a prominent place in their minds when the time comes to purchases within the category.

An important effect of digital media has been to blur, and in many senses collapse, both the difference between the promise and the product, and, in another dimension, the gap in time and space between the point at which we become interested in a purchase, the moment when we make the commitment, and from there, the experience of use.

The long-standing distinction between the shopper and the consumer, for example, has been dramatically altered by the ecommerce revolution. We buy from home or out and about, often in the context of use, and as a result, the behaviours of purchase and consumption fold into each other.

The thinking, the language, and the way brand communications are planned, have needed to change. This is, in large part, the origin of the current emphasis on customer experience.

Brands have rightly come to understand that, in digital markets, far from their equity residing primarily in relatively successful communication campaigns and tactics, where creative and media work together to craft and deliver appropriate, brand-positive messages, the promise and the experience – the communication and the product, if you like – have now become so closely integrated as to become one activity.

The medium has conclusively become the message.

Moving to the screen

While marketers are clear that such brand experience is typically spread across a range of touchpoints – and customer journeys, with ever-increasing sophistication and complexity, are planned and built accordingly into what are currently termed omni-channel models of engagement – much of the mindset and discipline of experience is derived from the technology-led discipline of user experience, or UX.

As customers have come to spend more time looking for, comparing, configuring and purchasing an ever-wider range and number of products and services online and now via mobile, first marketing and sales, and then fulfilment and service, have moved significantly onto the screen.

This was, in early days, if only for reasons of bandwidth, hardware capability and of course, the relative unsophistication of users themselves, an experience that was painfully poor. The pioneers of ecommerce were notoriously hamstrung by unintuitive interfaces, widespread session and basket abandonment, and a torrent of weary complaints.

Any meaningful improvement during this period was a reason for celebration, for both brands and customers.

As ecommerce became mainstream, the investment in experience went far deeper, to embrace business systems of all kinds. Amazon, to the frequent dismay of its shareholders, has always invested a disproportionate amount of revenue not merely into the optimization of the on-screen experience of consumers, but far deeper into the back end of its processes. These, as much as, if not more than, the screen interface, have driven its extraordinary levels of dependable, and not unusually delightful, service levels.

How could we go wrong? Surely continuing to invest in ever-greater levels of experience quality, across ever-wider areas of customer contact, is the most natural, the most certain strategy for innovation and, from there, growth?

This argument is both valid, and, as we saw earlier with transformation, not without continuing merit, as long as we understand that, in the turbulent context within which we now trade, today's efficiencies cannot be mistaken for, or, above all, stand in for, tomorrow's added value or growth.

Competing only on what are, typically, incremental improvements in customer experience is not, in the new context we've been considering, sufficient to guarantee growth in brand equity, customer purchasing, or loyalty.

Experience, to be blunt, does not build brands.

Whose experience is it?

As the quality of service across all channels stabilizes and standardizes, and as customers come to expect, not merely that this level be maintained, but that it be regularly improved upon and better integrated around their lives, their work, their time and their places, the centre of gravity inevitably and conclusively shifts.

What were previously 'point experiences', determined primarily by sector, by brand, by customer needs that were shaped around the industry structures of the suppliers or products and services, are becoming systematically, if not consistently or predictably, integrated, to form a 'circle of service' that surrounds the customer.

It's essential that we fully appreciate the implications of this shift.

We tend to assume, referring back to a time when it was culturally the case, that the business is providing an experience – a distinct, ownable encounter with the brand – to a customer whose function, in turn, is assumed to be a consumer of the experience.

The underlying belief here is that it is, in effect, the brand's experience that is delivered to the customer. That the enterprise is, therefore, in some sort of control. This is no longer a useful way of looking at a brand's role in the market, nor the impact of customer experience.

The reality of the interface between brand and consumer has conclusively changed.

Share of pizza

A seemingly frivolous metaphor is helpful here.

We see ourselves as delivering a unique, personalized pizza of experience to the customer. It's our pizza – we made it, after all – and we sell it, directly or otherwise, to them.

But in fact, the experience pizza now belongs to the customer. And it's divided into many thin slices.

Each of these slices represents what we might call 'a domain of customer concern'. These domains, to date, may have mapped more or less neatly across sectors: financial services, household goods, media and communications, healthcare and so on. This, as we know, is changing among the sectors that are more exposed to disruption, and as more integrated services cross sector boundaries, exploiting the well understood lowering of previous barriers to entry.

A number of enterprises currently occupy their chosen sector/slices quite comfortably. Some have been disrupted, thrown right off the pizza, or their share of slice dramatically reduced.

Some – very few incumbents so far, it needs to be admitted – have managed to grow their slices, perhaps at the expense of others, perhaps by identifying and developing a new proposition.

Many brands, at the lower end of the pizza scale, may represent no more than an olive or a piece of pineapple.

While this may offend the ego – who wants to be an olive, after all? – these may be respectable, indeed highly profitable businesses with a defensible offer that has plenty of growth potential.

They are, on the downside, often stuck on a single slice, with arguably little potential for horizontal expansion across customer domains or sectors.

A small number of very large competitors represent layers that cover most or even all of the experience pizza. They stretch across a wide range of slices, to the point where some have become more or less intrinsic to the whole pizza.

The network giants – who are, as time shows, uniquely and increasingly equipped to aggregate and integrate customer services across a potentially increasing range of domains – are able to reach across market sectors to exploit their pervasive and persistent dominance of types and volumes of data, customer attention, reach and depth.

So Google, Apple, Facebook, Amazon and their in-heritors come to define and control what seem like over-whelming dimensions of service innovation and value. Their utter dominance – in terms of sheer scale, control, and of course future potential growth – enables them to more or less define entire layers of customer experience at a global level.

But all this power and growth potential notwithstanding, the experience still belongs entirely and exclusively to the customer.

The integration of value

Having understood this, we clearly need to reframe the role and value of managed customer experience in build-ing, defending and growing brands and the enterprises that own them.

With a final, and, I admit, relieved last look back at the pizza metaphor, we can see that to define and evolve the parameters of the experiences we offer our customers on the isolated basis of an assumed brand journey, or even more broadly, sector imperatives, is to fail to grasp the current reality.

At the heart of the model is a customer, around whom a virtual infinity of optional products, services, and experiences, now revolves. They are no longer bound by the need to engage with a particular brand, within a particular sector, in order to meet a particular need.

The services they come to most value, over time, are those that usefully integrate other services that span and join up their respective domains, and the industry sectors that have traditionally, in the past, met those needs.

The only experience, in the end, that matters to them is the optimized, empowered, facilitated and ever-more streamlined experience of living a life that is increasingly rich in options, diverse in innovation, and as little frustrated by obstacles as possible.

Customer centricity

There is plenty of quite useful work happening under the title of 'customer centricity'. Again, there is a logic that on the surface feels both unarguable and reassuring.

How can we go wrong by sticking close to our customers, especially, to look back to seminal one to one marketing thinking, those that represent the most value to the enterprise?

The paradox here, as I hope we can see from the argument above, is that the model of wrapping brand experiences around the customer, to anticipate and meet their current and emerging needs with compelling, best in class experiences, is again too close to magical thinking.

The reality is, as the more challenging marketing academics have come to insist, that customers – most of all consumers in B2C markets – simply do not care nearly as much about our brands as we would wish (Byron Scott, author of the very valuable book *How Brands Grow* is particularly astringent on this subject).

Few customers want to have 'brand exclusive' experiences wrapped around them, except in the still-rare instances where the services in question offer what we might call a 'meta-layer' of experience that, eventually, will come to override and subsume the isolated, secondary offerings of sector-specific enterprises.

A good service always trumps a good product. A better

– and here we mean customized, aggregated and above all, intelligently integrated – service, will always appeal most to today's and tomorrow's unsentimental, rather ruthless, customers. The implications for companies doubling down on customer experience are stark.

In the absence of a sophisticated, costly service integration, that by definition must extend out of individual sectors to play a significant, if not always leading, role in experiences that span multiple customer domains, we are investing in the delivery of experiences that can only partially satisfy customers.

In this context, to expect any forms of customer-centric strategy, any experience design work that is rooted in one brand, trapped in a single sector, to significantly grow our businesses and the brands that serve them, is dangerously naive.

We are, in the end, like stubborn advertisers, demanding precious customer attention with too little of value to offer in return.

The invisible brand

Before we move on, there is a final dimension that needs

to be anticipated, further highlighting the urgent need to sharply differentiate experience design from service value.

As the Internet of Things, which we'll look at more closely in a later chapter, begins to impact life and work, many of the services for which we currently turn to the screen will become fully automated, and the corresponding opportunities to get screen time with customers will systematically diminish.

Trends such as the automated replenishment of household goods (already in evidence in Amazon's recent pushes into domestic shopping applications), and the increasing integration of health, lifestyle and dietary data and services (fitness and diet apps are proliferating and integrating more all the time), all point towards the growing appeal of services that either remove or minimize painful legwork, or automatically enhance experiences that are desirable, sometimes both.

Such services, we should note, significantly upset the applecart of consumer attention to brands.

By delivering high degrees of utility, while demanding nothing more than an initial configuration, and eventually not even that brief engagement with a brand, information-enabled services are, paradoxically, offering ever-increasing degrees of service value, while removing the element of active customer experience altogether.

As we might say, the customer's 'return on attention' here is unprecedented.

But how, in any established sense, do such automated and ultimately invisible services build brands?

We can be sure of one thing. The few enterprises that are able to aggressively invest in such offerings will, with luck, take up positions in their chosen markets that will be hard to shake.

Why would a consumer, for example, ever want to change their brand of toilet paper when, with automated replenishment, they never have to run out, or have to forget to add it to a shopping list again? And let's not forget, they would never have to pay attention to another loo paper advertisement for the rest of their lives. Lifetime toilet paper value ... there's a thought.

Surely the writing is on the wall. In the absence of any deeply strategic and disruptive – not to mention complex and costly – cross-sector service integration, without a willingness to firmly walk away from marketing's long-standing addiction to customer attention, experience design, exactly as we have come to understand digital transformation, represents in isolation no solid defence against turbulence.

We must look further, in particular now focusing on how value moves across the domains and sectors we touched on above, in order to catch sight of solid strategic ground.

Chapter summary

- Customer experience is a central and ongoing requirement but does not, in isolation, build brands;

- The experience is not provided by the brand – it is owned by the customer, and brands may or may not usefully contribute to it;

- The network giants are able to connect sectors and services to aggregate, integrate and own dominant share of experience, to which individual brand offerings are secondary;

- As services become further integrated across sectors and increasingly automated, customers will gravitate to brands that replace targeted communications with intelligent services that demand little attention but provide high value.

The innovation trap

4

Defining and evaluating innovation in context •
cultural tension in the enterprise in the absence
of strategic focus • how innovation affects value •
moving away from making isolated bets.

Innovation without context

In the previous two chapters, we have reframed the roles
of the two most prominent enterprise responses to the
chronic uncertainty amongst leadership that our increasingly disruptive environment has created: digital business
transformation and customer experience management.

This leaves us in an uncomfortable state of deep quandary. Where are the workable strategic alternatives? From
here we will work towards a fresh and, if not free of uncertainty, at least tangible and comprehensible model of the
turbulent business context.

However, before moving on to explore the root causes of this uncertainty, we need to briefly examine, and then proceed to put into a more robust and critical context, the third touchstone: innovation.

So much has been and continues to be written on this familiar subject, that to avoid repetition, we will dwell only briefly on it here.

While the core questions of how innovation should work, its relative impacts, and in particular its relationship to future value remain, for now, ungrounded, every business is, in one form or another, more or less centrally concerned with it.

But what, exactly, are we talking about?

There is an unhelpful plethora of definitions of innovation, and it is surely central to enterprise strategy that we be crystal clear on what we actually mean, in order to set a foundation for confident and productive commitment to what are, inevitably, increasingly important programmes. It's especially important, as we have seen with both transformation and experience, given the degrees of expectation and investment represented.

Within any enterprise, there is a common and pervasive cultural tension that is exposed by any innovation project, in particular revolving around the matter of relative impact on value, and of course, relative return on investment.

This is the familiar stuff of legend. Change leaders, the most vocal promoters of the new, line up against financial leaders, alongside, inevitably, the defenders of the old way.

The core issue is that the premises on which the argument is fought are frequently deeply unclear. We don't agree on what we're investing in, we don't agree why; perhaps worst of all, we don't have a tangible shared idea of what value we're creating. In other words, the context for the innovation is far too elusive for comfort.

The evangelistic St Johns are as much of a problem here as the Doubting Thomases.

For the former, the commitment to the future that innovation programmes represent is not up for serious debate: something, surely has to change, and we are finding our way, albeit experimentally, into the future. This underlying belief – 'Because we actually have no choice …' – is, if anything, more inflammatory to the debate.

For the latter, leaving aside the natural organizational and individual resistance to change of any kind that is intrinsic to most human beings, the lack of familiar models of return on investment (exactly how will this thing pay for itself?) combined with a not-unfounded suspicion of the new and shiny, renders any such investment at best questionable and, at worst, irrational.

This tension is, of course, fully part of the challenge of managing a modern corporate culture. No amount of internal rhetoric, nor any declared leadership commitment to a bold and courageous push into the future, will entirely remove it.

But we see how problematic and divisive the lack of a foundational definition, one that delineates what we do and, just as important, do not mean by innovation, can be.

Definition and evaluation

Paddy Miller and Thomas Wedell-Wedellsborg, in their useful book *Innovation As Usual: How to help your people bring great ideas to life*, have dug deep to provide what is for me the most useful – in terms of both precision and application – way of framing the subject.

They define innovation as simply 'getting results by doing different things'.

Beneath this superficially child-like phrase lies a core distinction; perhaps we can think of it as a manifesto. It's certainly a genuine challenge.

Following their logic, if our programmes of innovation either fail to get results, or fall back onto some familiar form of business as usual, they are not, in fact, usefully 'innovative'.

Putting aside what constitutes 'doing different things' – there are now so many options arriving in our inboxes every day that we have no shortage of new things to consider – the focus needs surely to be on how we envisage, frame and above all, evaluate 'results'.

This is where the innovation buck, no matter how exciting the technology or commercial potential may seem, abruptly stops.

It's the widespread inability to place any innovation in context, to answer that most basic of questions, 'Compared to what, exactly?', that causes these programmes – upon which we rely so heavily to enable and create the new forms of value that will pull the enterprise to safety and into a productive future – to aggravate the very uncertainty that we hope they will reduce.

Until we are able to frame and agree upon a robust context for innovation value – its real impact on customer and enterprise value – and notwithstanding the importance and urgency to 'do something, anything …' that drives the overall need, we are, in fact working not with innovations at all: we are doing not much more than making bets on promising but isolated inventions.

As we've already seen with transformation and experience, in the absence of a workable model within which to frame this value, we are putting the future of the enterprise in danger. To perhaps a less dramatic extent, the same limitation applies to innovation.

Further, until any innovation finds its place on The Network and is optimally integrated into an ecosystem where it can offer and balance value for both customer and enterprise, it remains nothing more than a promising invention.

With this in mind, a fresh understanding of the overall dynamics of The Network is central to determining, at every level, the potential impact of, and thus the appropriate level of investment in, any innovation opportunity.

To usefully recontextualize these challenges, and to move towards the principles of a viable enterprise response to our uncertainty regarding future value, we need to get to grips with what drives the chronic turbulence of the environment.

We turn now to examine the dynamics of The Network,

which emerge as the true source of the chronic turbulence from which we are suffering.

Chapter summary

- A consistent and unified enterprise commitment to innovation is impossible without clear definition and context;

- The lack of an articulated and broadly accepted strategic framework leaves innovation programmes stranded, unable to impact customer and enterprise value;

- Until innovations are fully contextualized both within the business, and in their optimal location on The Network, they remain inventions whose value remains latent.

Network disruption

5

The expanding universe of The Network •
disruption by the network giants • separating
disruption cause and effect • fixed value chains
become fluid ecosystems • The Network itself as
primary disruptor.

Introducing Network Dynamics

With few significant exceptions, value, along with the work
that creates it, has moved onto The Network, by which I
mean here the universal flow of communication and information across the effectively infinite, and increasingly integrated, millions of networks of all kinds, including physical
ones.

Like any universe, this one is constantly expanding, and
yet the rules that govern that shift, and that would make it
in some manner predictable, remain obscure and daunting.

We have already touched on how the constant acceleration of movement on The Network, in parallel with the continuous increase in the volume of data that it carries, makes decision quality, in the context of our search for strategic certainty, impossible.

The nature of these changes is the source of our growing uncertainty, anathema to the leadership of any enterprise. We are not, as yet, adequately equipped to make confident decisions about how to approach the future.

The Internet, or rather its progenitor, ARPANET, was deliberately designed to find its way around obstacles.

As long as we are frustrated in finding viable, and in the end, profitable ways in which to participate in The Network's torrent of potential value, we are in danger of becoming increasingly passive, or, worse, 'dead nodes'. We are, we could say, at constant and increasing risk of excommunication.

A number of well-known sector disruptors seem, at first glance, to have found short cuts to unbelievable success.

Naturally, we are keen to grasp how they have apparently decoded the new dynamics that have driven them – with unprecedented speed, scale and valuations – to what seem like effortless positions of dominance.

As we'll come to see, the quite similar philosophies that these giant disruptors have adopted do not, in themselves, hold the magic key.

They are all propelled by the power and speed of The Network. And it's The Network itself, in fact, that is the great disruptor. In other words, the medium itself has become both riveting opportunity and relentless threat.

The network giants

We can't discuss the disruptive present and future without looking more closely at the network giants. They symbolize everything that's exciting and intimidating about the digital horizon.

At the time of writing, the so-called NATU cluster – Netflix, Airbnb, Tesla and Uber – is discussed everywhere, every day. And these companies have arrived on the backs of this century's original disruptors, GAFA – Google, Apple, Facebook and Amazon.

In just five years, Uber grew to achieve in 2015 a valuation of over $50 billion dollars. Pretty good for a taxi company! But Uber isn't just the world's largest taxi company. It's not, except in the most basic sense, in the taxi business at all.

We need to understand that the network disruptors are not, in themselves, the causes of profound change. Like the other giant network disruptors – and there will be plenty more – they represent just a few of a range of symptoms.

What's most challenging about all the network giants is not their scale, their growth, their domination of existing categories, and their bold creation of entirely new ones. It's the underlying dynamic that drives them. These are only the first disruptive enterprises to take full advantage of the dynamics of The Network.

Think about Google's PageRank algorithm. Larry Page and Sergey Brin realized that the relevance of a particular webpage was best calculated not by the content of the page itself. It was the performance of the webpage on the network – who had found it, who had used it, who'd linked to it, and how many times – that mattered.

We were searching and finding content. But the service that delivered it – and continues to do so, with more powerful and sophisticated applications and services regularly emerging – was built on a breakthrough understanding of the new context.

In other words, it was Network Dynamics that created Google.

From passive to active network

This is not the network we used to know: the passive land-scape of railways, roads, boxes and wires; the linear distribution and communication that drove the Industrial Age.

It is an active, chaotic, unfamiliar cultural and commercial phenomenon. A new place to live, to work and to do business. Above all, The Network has its own dynamics. We could say ... 'It's Alive!'

Michael Porter's venerable value chain – with its comforting model of predictable, incremental competitive advantage – is turned rudely on its head by Network Dynamics. It is being replaced by fast-moving, fluid and uncertain ecosystems. These are coming to define how markets work, and how enterprises compete. In fact, who survives, and who grows.

The traditional idea of firms creating and building new value and then shipping it across physical and communications networks suddenly feels very last century, because value now lives, alongside billions of connected consumers, on The Network itself.

Our network giants all operate variants of a single model. The more we look at it, the more we can see just how very disruptive it is. We could say that, far from creating value internally, and then delivering it through market channels, they have learned to harvest value *from* The Network.

Stop and think for a second how truly disruptive this is: the established model of value creation and exploitation is conclusively reversed.

Their ability to develop, place and continually evolve their algorithms on The Network is what enables them to first disrupt and then dominate their target sectors.

It also enables them to jump into entirely new sectors.

Such potential further disruption is based not merely on the traditional access points that, say, an established and extensible manufacturing base or brand dominance of a particular sector might confer, but any appealing market opportunity where their customer base, their service capabilities, and of course, their growing power and reach, can be easily combined and exploited.

This further ratchets up the threat that both current and emerging network disruptors represent to incumbents: their ability to move on an opportunity is not based on previous rules of sector competency, entry barriers or opportunity cost.

The more the work and the value shift onto The Network, the more market dominance, fast innovation and ruthless competition are possible.

Network uncertainty

The strategic implications, as we start to look over the digital horizon, are revolutionary.

This is the disruption that needs our attention. Sector disruptors will come and go. But until we understand the true source of the challenge, the context that throws up both opportunity and threat, we will be looking in the wrong place for answers.

To reiterate, it's The Network itself that is the great disruptor.

The sector disruptors on which so much focus is currently placed have lessons for us only insofar as they force us to put down our previous ways of thinking, of doing strategy in the hunt for fresh customer and enterprise value on the assumption that changes are only occurring in particular markets, affecting one sector or another.

Underneath the surface, the chronic disruption that The Network represents, that occasionally tosses up these admittedly remarkable new enterprises, is sector-agnostic.

To be very clear, whatever changes – in particular, whatever entrants – may emerge to disrupt certain of the more vulnerable sectors within the business environment, we need to think of these as merely superficial waves.

It's the underlying tides that we need to understand. Unfortunately, at least until we learn to somehow work within and around them, these seismic movements will continue to evade any form of prediction or even adequate diagnosis.

As long as this is the case, to look to frame our strategic decisions on the basis of evidence from the past informing hypotheses about the present and future, is a philosophy that is, unfortunately, no longer viable.

We must seek to become masters of the new uncertainty.

To begin to understand the implications and to reframe strategy and, ultimately, enterprise structure, we now need to take a step back and examine how the nature, creation, control and distribution of value itself have been steadily pulled apart by The Network over the past three decades.

Chapter summary

- The Network is continuously expanding and accelerating;

- The network giants are not the causes but the effects of Network Dynamics;

- The Network is a fully active environment that is, as a result, constantly producing 'latent value' that the network giants are learning to harvest – a complete reversal of traditional business models;

- We need to understand the underlying dynamics – without this insight, sector disruptors in themselves have little to teach us.

Value disruption

6

Radical shifts in power • how information
overturned the package holiday • the unpicking
of value chains • the new market makers • a
revolution in value.

Shifts in power

We now dig into the origins of the disruption that The Network fosters, looking at the history of how information itself has steadily unpicked previously robust and reassuring value chains, leaving behind chaotic, and frequently incumbent-hostile, ecosystems.

It's worth noting two points, which ground our argument in a history that will feel immediately recognizable, and demonstrate the historic causes of the doubt and uncertainty that enterprise leadership now faces.

First, this process preceded both the Internet and the

cellular networks by over a decade. It was the digitization and democratization of data, enabled and driven by the PC explosion of the 1980s that introduced the destructive impact of information to the market.

Second, as the leading documenter of The Network, Manuel Castells, has so thoroughly articulated and proven in his studies and published work, this same process initiated the subsequently unstoppable transfer of power from business to customer.

It is this cultural shift that has, in turn, thrown up so many challenges to the enterprise. After all, whoever has the power has the ability to decide what is and is not of value and to what degree.

The unbundling of the package holiday

About 25 years ago, the long-established, valuable packaged holiday business began to be unbundled.

A small but determined form of consumer power entered the market, nourished by a new depth and richness of information and propelled by equally new computing technologies.

Gigantic holiday brochures would thump onto doormats

everywhere soon after New Year, as their production shifted from laboured cut-and-paste to database and desktop publishing. There was sector-wide introduction of an often-forgotten interactive tool, the customer call-centre.

Holiday purchasers, thus equipped and empowered, began to tweak the rules, swapping the jet-ski for the karaoke or perhaps the extra bedroom for the beachside location.

The packaged holiday business had always relied entirely upon a rigid framework of services: a tightly wound value chain made up of volume, discount and perhaps above all, minimal management costs. A well-oiled, while rarely luxurious, production line of sea, sun, sand and sangria.

So this new, informed customer choice introduced cost and complexity. Eventually, it came to threaten and then dismantle the value chain itself.

The holiday industry eventually bowed to the pressure, and very soon, fresh choice and flexibility – accompanied by an unfamiliar feeling that times were, profoundly, beginning to change – entered the picture.

From direct access to airline and hotel booking systems, through the explosion of budget flights, across to opinion sites like TripAdvisor, information has, on one hand, utterly transformed the consumer experience of leisure travel, and on the other, dismantled the structure, margins, security and predictability of the industry.

We should note, in passing, that it was the parallel obsessive unpicking and reassembly of the air travel value chain that enabled the disruptive travel and services entrepreneur Stelios Haji-Ioannou to pioneer the wafer-thin margins that launched easyJet.

How information disrupts markets

What followed, as the Web took hold of this dynamic and sent it around the world, was not just about the now-familiar list of enabling technologies, entrepreneurial success stories and spectacular crashes.

The effect was to shift not merely the language of value, but first the distribution, and then, most compellingly, the very creation of significant amounts of value, from business, via The Network, across to increasingly connected customers.

Information, driven by an explosion of processing power and connectedness, has since transformed the business environment and replicated the case of package holidays across all kinds of sectors.

Imagine a vice – the sort you'd find on a workbench. A big one, with customers on one side, and the new network giants, such as Google and Facebook, surrounded by a rapidly expanding cloud of customer service innovators, on the other.

These two sides have, since the late 1990s, evolved an entirely symbiotic relationship. I give you a steady flow of transformative service innovations, you give me your attention, your loyalty and your advocacy. The more you give me, the more I'm able to invest in the next wave of empowering value.

Google – the company that so rapidly overturned the $500bn business of advertising – launched with the simplest of web pages, whose white background and single search box epitomized pure consumer centricity.

Alongside its revolutionary PageRank algorithm, it was an obsession with consumer value – then mostly unconditional, somewhat altruistic, certainly magical – that built the house of Google. And its explosive constituency of millions upon millions of daily users rewarded it in kind.

Over time – and it's happened very, very fast – the two sides of this vice have pulled closer together, exerting an irresistible and destructive pressure on the industries caught between them.

Music initially attracted much of the publicity as file-sharing – perhaps the first globally acknowledged exercise in customers' flexing of their new power over incumbent enterprises – began the process of unpicking what had previously been an unassailable (notwithstanding the comparatively minor headache of manufactured piracy) command of entertainment value.

But looking more closely, we see that all media-related businesses, marketing services, healthcare, banking and financial services, real estate and plenty more have felt the cold breath of information on their necks. Most recently, retail has been suffering from 'show rooming', where consumers browse in the comfort of a store, then use smartphones to get instant price comparisons with ecommerce sites.

Unstable value chains

Imagine classic value chains – they look like lines of boxes with a point at the customer end – being squeezed in the same way as we saw the package holiday being unbundled.

Under this increasing pressure, segments begin to pop out of the value chain. And the problem with value chains is that they're rather like dominoes. Once one piece goes down, the fragility of the structure takes over.

The sector in question, under pressure from all that information, devolves from being a stable value chain, or set of value chains, to becoming a hostile ecosystem. Relationships are disrupted, margins are eroded, logistics are pulled apart. Uncertainty begins to bite hard.

While it's the chain that is broken up, it's the value that falls away, like old cement, as the bricks of previously robust business models are prised apart by information wielded by networked customers. And these customers are of course empowered by the Goliaths of the online era, the network disruptors.

Power over value

Category killers such as Google, Amazon, eBay, Expedia and Facebook share one crucial, rarely recognized attribute.

They each provide connected consumers with a different 'sense-making window' into the chaotic ecosystems that The Network has created in dismantling, one by one, the industries most exposed to the corrosion of information. In a sense, they enable consumers to construct their own personal value chains.

The technology giants are the market makers – indeed, the kingmakers – of the entire online economy. They have taken the lost commercial value of the fractured value chains that information deconstructed and flipped it across into the willing hands of billions of connected consumers.

By selling market access back to incumbents in the form of digital advertising, and, in the case of Amazon, a ruthlessly customer-sided and cost-controlled retail outlet, the network giants have not only disrupted and come to dominate their chosen areas of competition. They have gone on to become powerful gatekeepers of the very markets they have overturned.

The immediate implication on the business side is huge: not only do the location and control of value need revisiting, but the very nature of value itself comes into question.

Asking 'what business are we in now?' is rarely a frivolous question today.

Chapter summary

- Over several decades, the explosion and democratization of information have picked apart a series of stable sector value chains, to replace them with chaotic ecosystems;

- The network giants have both built and been built upon the technologies, products and services that exploit this radical shift in the nature, creation and distribution of value;

- The Network's growth and acceleration are driving this effect across all susceptible sectors.

Liquid objects

7

Understanding the Internet of Things • the IoT in
historical and cultural context • the key concept of
decisionality • beyond wearable technologies • the
potential effects on brands and branding.

A very big idea

Like so many techno-cultural shifts in waiting, the Internet
of Things (IoT) is today as widely misrepresented as it is
vigorously discussed.

What we do know is that intelligent, automated and
widely distributed services will significantly disrupt our
relationships with our technologies, with our physical environments and with our bodies. From this angle it's easy
to see how the IoT can shake up the very culture within
which businesses and brands either survive and thrive, or
are disrupted and overcome.

Unlike every previous global technology wave, most of the key elements for this seismic shift are already present, familiar to us and fairly evenly distributed.

This perfect storm will not touch down on every coast of our lives at the same time, in many cases not even in the same decade.

But the evidence to date suggests we will soon enough see startling instances of 'creative destruction' that can't be entirely envisioned from where we stand today.

A closer look

What, exactly, *is* the Internet of Things?

There are many variants and nuances of interpretation, however a respectable layman's definition comes from Wikipedia:

The Internet of Things (IoT, sometimes Internet of Everything) is the network of physical objects or 'things' embedded with electronics, software, sensors, and connectivity to enable objects to exchange data with the manufacturer, operator and/or other connected devices based on the infrastructure of International Telecommunication Union's Global Standards Initiative.

The Internet of Things allows objects to be sensed and controlled remotely across existing network infrastructure, creating opportunities for more direct integration between the physical world and computer-based systems, and resulting in improved efficiency, accuracy and economic benefit. Each thing is uniquely identifiable through its embedded computing system but is able to interoperate within the existing Internet infrastructure. Experts estimate that the IoT will consist of almost 50 billion objects by 2020.

This summarizes for us, very broadly, the structure of the technology.

But what difference will the Internet of Things make? What does it mean?

We can anticipate three significant and eventually radical shifts that will sweep across life, culture and business.

1. We can expect to rapidly, economically and automatically track and respond to changes in the physical world, in the same manner that we have become so accustomed to doing in the virtual one.

2. Those changes will be incorporated into intelligent sys-

tems that will, in turn, make decisions about (a) whether to respond to a change and (b) if so, in what way.

3. And finally, this process will be distributed and federated, so that we can access and exploit this new, powerful intelligence, anyhow, anywhere, anytime.

The Internet of Things is in fact a vision, an idea whose time has clearly come. That said, its intrinsic complexity is painfully obvious.

The difficulty in deciding both what we mean and the nature of its potential.

The widely varying evaluations of its commercial impact.

The familiar tension between the enthusiasm of those who see radical, science fiction-like shifts in life, work and culture, vs. the understandable concerns of those who see a quantum leap in threats to data privacy.

Above all, the struggle to discover ways of framing the value impacts and implications for businesses, for brands, and for customers.

These are the challenges that the IoT poses.

To get our arms around it, and to begin to articulate exactly why and where our focus, our analysis, and in the end, our investment should be placed, we first need to place the IoT in simple, pragmatic historical, technological and cultural context.

A long history of clever things

We have been building intelligence into the physical world for centuries.

Think of the kettle that whistles when it boils. A primitive mechanical sensor responds to a certain volume of steam passing through it, to create a sound when the water boils.

Add electricity, and we have the kettle that switches it-self off: still one of the most pervasive and useful sensors, the thermostat. Pull on this thread long enough, and we arrive at Google's intelligent, learning Nest device for the home.

Add processing power to the electric kettle (with a nod to the timed coffee maker on our way past) and we reach the Nespresso machine, which has enough intelligence to – every time – deliver coffee of barista quality.

Notice one more thing. We move, as we advance from the mechanical, through the electrical, to the electronic, from manufactured product through to enabling service. We see how 'the work that gets done' shifts, in parallel with an important empowering effect that control over such automated services confers on the user.

It's about the power, before it's about the value.

Power over our environment, the objects (including our own physical bodies) that occupy it, and above all, power over the way information and objects are increasingly able to usefully interact, without incurring work for the user, to offer services that transform the ways in which new value is both created and experienced.

An age of context

It's useful to think of the cultural and commercial impacts of The Network in three sequential waves.

At its inception in the mid-90s, the Web aspired to universal connectedness. 'Are you on the Internet?' was a very common question at the time: now this seems rather quaint.

Prior to that revolutionary period, activity on the Internet outside its original military and academic purposes was restricted to CompuServe news groups and unwieldy lists, painstakingly maintained by unpaid rebels with a plethora of causes. But increasingly, both homes and offices resounded with the unforgettable grind and squeal of dial-up modems. This was the age of America Online.

Soon enough, richer forms of material squeezed their way into the rapidly broadening pipes of the Web. Our on-line experience was utterly transformed by the introduction of broadband. At the same time, content was being added to connection.

The corporate milestone for this time was surely the extraordinary, and ultimately disastrous, merger in January 2000 of AOL with Time Warner.

Despite that sobering bump in the road, content is still front and centre in every brand, every agency and every publishing business in the world.

What's more, the smartphones, app stores, high-speed (and of course, programmatic) networks that are the current state of the media union, do nothing better than ship content of all kinds to the world.

However, hidden in every one of those same rich content-carrying smartphones, is a handful of sensors, each one of which has the remarkable ability to convert the physical world to digital signals. It's these sensors, most of all their superhuman ability to pick up and communicate, in microseconds, changes of all kinds, that set up the third wave of the Web.

From here, it's very much about the context. The Network embraces connectedness and content and pulls them together to once again revolutionize the paradigm. Such distributed intelligence builds a new landscape of personal, real time services. No longer just digital tools that are there when you ask for them, these are becoming pervasive, vigilant, and invisible helpers, dotted throughout our physical world.

This is why we refer, inadequately, to the Internet of Things.

Arriving at this next contextual wave of The Network, we could say we've completed our mission in cyberspace, where we played for some 20 years with data, with connectedness, with our new power over interactive content.

As we come back to a smarter, 'instrumented' physical life, what sort of changes can we expect?

Extended 'decisionality'

We've looked at three waves of network evolution that have carried us from new kinds of empowering connectedness, through to now, where we come to expect increasing sophistication and impact in contextual value.

There are three more, parallel, waves of empowerment that are critical to our full appreciation of the effect of the IoT. The introduction of information technology has evolved along a clear trajectory. It has enabled decisioning at three levels: the human level, the system level, and most recently, as the IoT begins to emerge, at the object (and also environment and product) level.

It has been the development and growth of The Network – in the form of the Internet in its various manifestations – that has propelled the recent stages of this evolution.

1. People first making better, more complex decisions and taking actions faster, enabled by computer systems with minimal networking;

2. Decisions and actions then being enabled in networked computer systems;

3. Decisions and actions now becoming enabled in the physical world by places, things and products. This represents the most pragmatic view of the role, meaning and potential value of the Internet of Things.

Understanding the IoT in the context of this new 'decisionality', as being about not merely the location and connection of things on networks, but the rapid extension of intelligence to environment, object, product and service level, we come to comprehend the nature of the shift.

When we look at both consumer and enterprise value through the fresh lens of decisionality, and in particular when we are able to bring the resulting insights together to develop new models of value exchange, our ability to understand and leverage the transformative power of the Internet of Things is dramatically unlocked.

Customer value and decisionality

It's no coincidence that, for now, the IoT-based products that excite most consumer press are wearables, sensors that detect physical changes – in our environments and in our bodies – and process them to bring us a rapidly expanding blend of personal services.

With our diet and fitness apps, our adaptive thermo-stats, and let's not forget satnav (one of the most trans-formative innovations of all time, in itself a compelling example of how the IoT enables us to more easily and comprehensively manage our physical lives with tools built purely on data) we're brought right down to earth, landing with a bump back in our own bodies.

We've heard plenty of talk about the Quantified Self, the trend towards personal instrumentation. But what's interesting here is not just quantification, counting footsteps and calories. When this personal and contextual data is married to ever-smarter and further-reaching algorithms, it's the quality and tone of life itself that changes.

The Internet of Things already tells us about ourselves in far greater detail than we ourselves could ever do.

When we combine the data from what we do, with what's happening around us, then present them in real time to powerful algorithms that process and extract from that raw, often mundane input, narratives of struggle, progress, personal triumph – or maybe just a smaller heating bill – our mediated world shifts on its axis.

'Just done it'

The longest-running icon for consumer value in IoT is, of course, Nike+, first unveiled, originally in close partnership with Apple, on May 20th 2006, and later evolved to become Fuelband.

The user appeal of the service is simple. It applies a

variety of basic sensors to capture quite primitive information about a runner's speed, acceleration, location and elevation. These are processed and presented back both during the run (mainly as audio) and far more richly afterwards, when easy to grasp and easy to share infographics are automatically ported to any screen.

Nike+ takes data from the traditionally isolated sport of distance running, and presents it back to its users and their connected friends, as ongoing narratives of personal triumph and transformation. This is, to paraphrase Le Corbusier, first of all 'a machine for storytelling'.

Nike+ (not forgetting its many descendants) confers fresh, addictive power on the consumer through data and algorithm. And if the service has led the way into day-to-day, commoditized IoT, we must accept that this new kind of brand engagement takes us far from advertised messaging – 'the promise followed by the product' – to profoundly different brand behaviours.

This brings us to an area of core leadership concern.

What happens to brands when, on the one hand, their key role in culture as guardians of customer meaning is directly exposed to chronic turbulence, and on the other, an increasing range and number of the key communications touchpoints through which brand communications are delivered become subsumed by the sort of intelligent, automated and invisible customer services promised by the IoT?

Chapter summary

- The Internet of Things lands The Network back in the physical world, and pulls objects, environments, products and services into its orbit;

- This dynamic further impacts and accelerates the shift of power to customers;

- The paradigm for understanding the cultural and commercial impacts of the IoT is 'extended decisionality' – the movement of value and the work that produces it from human, to system and then into the connected physical world;

- Nike+ has been a powerful, well-established signpost for this new model of value, building strong equity by replacing brand communications with intelligence, empowering service.

Liquid living

8

Lessons from cultural and social theory •
understanding the effects of media technology
• changes in identity and belonging • individual
and social power • peak human experiences • the
collapse of time and place • connected isolation •
the co-creation of value.

Lessons from culture

Most of the insights that enterprises and their brands have
required over the decades have derived from the acute
observation of culture and society. The outputs may not
always have been startlingly fresh – quite often when presented with a fresh angle of brand opportunity, one's first
response is, well, didn't we know that already?

Brands – and the research companies that continue to
feed them with more information than they probably can

ever use – tend to live behind an analytical curtain, and while it is by no means the rule, sometimes we are reminded of the accountants who know the price of everything and the value of nothing.

And yet every now and then a profound, meaningful and resonant idea emerges, and life itself, at least in the markets touched by the brand, is transformed.

The icons of the last century or so have all had their moments in the creative sun. The communications work of global brands such as Volkswagen, both Nike and Adidas, of course Coca-Cola, Burberry and inevitably Apple, to mention just a familiar handful, have had direct impact on culture and thereby powerfully lifted their own commercial fortunes.

There's no doubt about the power of branding, and the corresponding importance of the communications that deliver it.

The dominion that the world's most powerful brands have exercised over meaning, trust, value, share of spend, and also identity and aspiration, is undeniable.

We've already looked in some detail at the changes in marketing strategy and practice that the digital revolution, and following that, the chronic market turbulence that The

Network will continue to propel, has effected.

But how have customers themselves changed, if indeed they have at all, in this context, and what are at least some of the key implications for the enterprise?

Voices of the masters

It's come to light, much to the surprise of far too many of us, that the human being formerly known as the customer or consumer no longer plays by many of the rules that we have traded on.

It's remarkable that so much of the science and thinking exploring and explaining these emerging behaviours has been embraced and indeed often lionized in academic circles, while being either determinedly ignored or hyper-selectively cherry-picked out of context in commerce.

On the basis that much of the most seminal and still relevant work on human experience, meaning, identity, social life, values and value has been done in the past half century or so by academics infinitely more qualified and focused than I, here we'll look briefly at a sample of the most salient thoughts from some of the brightest minds.

Having briefly examined and summarized a fraction of

their work on what it means to be a connected human, we'll explore the resulting implications for customer expectation and behaviour.

These are almost all thinkers from a tight cluster of disciplines, whose most enduring outputs have landed in culture, social or media theory.

While having needed for my own purposes to be something of a magpie in approaching what is a significant and often demanding body of combined work, I've found their outputs to be of immense and recurring value in interpreting the zeitgeist, as modernity has been propelled forward by The Network.

It should be noted that the snapshots of their work below do not represent anything more than a useful set of co-ordinates for us to draw with, in order to get to grips with just how – and how much – the customer of the present and future differs from the received wisdom.

In each case, therefore, I've also suggested a single book for readers who may wish to dig deeper.

Media as extensions of man

Marshall McLuhan is the most referenced and misquoted

visionary of life and culture on The Network. While his core body of work was published as far back as the 1960s, he was even back then answering – albeit often cryptically and playfully – fundamentally modern questions, many of which have yet to be formally asked.

His most penetrating and subtle lessons are often buried under his now-too-familiar 'global village' and 'medium is the message' insights.

McLuhan is an invaluable touchstone for the current and future world, of how emerging media technologies need to be understood not merely in terms of how they make more content available to more of the world over more channels, but how they rewire culture itself.

In particular, his description of media as 'extensions of man', fully articulated in the masterpiece of 1964, *Understanding Media*, needs our consideration.

For McLuhan, all technologies that extend the basic functions of the human mind and body are media; he looks far beyond the familiar channels of content and communication, to include the wheel, clothing, buildings and so on.

Note the difference. Where, particularly in marketing, we have been brought up to see media as originating, in a variety of forms, on the side of the enterprise, and pushed out to audiences and customers through a growing plethora of channels and devices, McLuhan explains the dynamic as entirely the reverse.

Media is, or are, as we should correctly say, a set of outbound phenomena, that originate with the individual.

Challenging thoughts, and tough to get our heads around of course. But McLuhan's sophisticated vision of media anticipates so much of what is now happening, at increasing speed, on The Network.

Whatever the limitations of customer centricity as a reaction to turbulence may be, a map of any market that places anything other than the customer at its heart is unlikely to reflect reality.

When we allow ourselves to remain trapped in a broadcast model of media – and this is very deeply entrenched in so many corners of enterprise thought and strategy – we miss, and miss out on, the origins of the shift in power to the customer, the real challenges faced by advertising as a builder of brands.

Above all, we root ourselves in a paradigm that is no longer useful, one where the content of all our media channels is seen as more important than the cultural effect of the technologies that carry it.

Identity and belonging

The challenges to meaning, to identity and, at the most elemental level, to what it feels like to be human in the modern age are well documented.

But these changes did not originate with the emergence of the digital world, nor are the subsequent impacts of The Network best understood by only referring to present day analysis. Social media, to pick a familiar example, cannot be fully grasped and incorporated into strategy solely by examining the current phenomena. Facebook and Twitter, in other words, are as much symptoms as they are causes.

The insights that thinkers such as Erving Goffman, in his highly influential book of 1959, *The Presentation of Self in Everyday Life*, offer, provide important and surprisingly fresh illuminations of the anthropological and cultural origins of what we tend to think of as intrinsically digital behaviours and trends.

In my opinion, Anthony Giddens, the eminent social theorist whose work spans a number of domains, including advising political leadership, dominates, for good reason, his discipline. An excellent introduction to Giddens' thought is *The Consequences of Modernity*, and to get more deeply – and I must say enjoyably – to grips with the relevant impacts of his work, *Self-Identity in Modernity* is invaluable.

Giddens has also written extensively, and with his customary depth and precision, about changes in the nature, location and dynamics of trust.

His body of work uniquely balances the authority and sure-footedness of a true expert, and a willingness to think about important matters in very different ways. He says:

A person's identity is not to be found in behaviour, nor – important though this is – in the reactions of others, but in the capacity to keep a particular narrative going. The individual's biography, if she is to maintain regular interaction with others in the day-to-day world, cannot be wholly fictive. It must continually integrate events which occur in the external world, and sort them into the ongoing 'story' about the self.

This sounds entirely familiar; furthermore it is such a fresh and concise account of the now-universal appeal of Facebook and its kin.

Individual and social power

A recurring theme in our argument so far has been the shifts in power that first the democratization of information, followed by the digital revolution, and now the turbulence of The Network have introduced to both culture and commerce.

Customers – people – now have their hands directly on a degree of agency inside the hitherto closed doors of society, business and politics that would have been unrecognizable 20 years ago.

The undisputed master of the dynamics that both drive and steer these extraordinary changes in the way we think, behave, come together and, equally, come apart is Manuel Castells. For decades he and his teams have meticulously dissected life and power on The Network. Alongside Giddens, I would argue that no other thinker combines such authority with such intellectual rigour and courage.

Castells is uniquely persuasive when focused on social changes on The Network. He writes of a 'Fifth Estate', a new aggregated force made up of individuals and groups who, due to their newfound connectedness, are able to unite and take action on behalf of shared issues of concern, without recourse to traditional institutions of power and their associated channels.

The best way into Castells' work is via the recent book, *Communications Power*, a typically exhaustive but still often exhilarating examination of these fundamental shifts in power across to connected individuals and tribes.

But be prepared. All of his work is so thoroughly thought through and researched that the reading can be a challenge.

The experience of Flow

I believe Steve Jobs' uncanny ability to read the mind of the connected consumer – far better even than they could themselves – was rooted in a seminal 1990 book, *Flow*.

Mihaly Csikszentmihalyi (pronounced Mee-hy Cheek-sent-ma-hy-ee, by the way) has carved a unique niche out of examining and articulating what makes us really happy.

His work has, as we'd expect from the title of the book, been co-opted by user and customer experience practitioners, but while this adoption has led to improvement in those disciplines, it misses the mark in terms of the point and impact of Csikszentmihalyi's most important thought.

When great artists, sportspeople, performers and, most importantly, people like you and I, encounter that all-too-rare, yet unforgettable experience of being 'in the zone', we have some of the most satisfying and uplifting times of our lives.

When we are in Flow, we feel entirely in control of our actions and, at the same time, are performing 'out of our skin'. So while it's easy to mistake Flow for a set of hygiene factors for the design of environment and experience, its real message is one of potential for personal transformation.

Why does this matter in the context of enterprise strategy in chronic turbulence? Simply because, I believe, our insight into and expectation of what constitutes profound fulfilment amongst human beings is calibrated far too low.

Rare brands such as Nike, Red Bull and perhaps a handful of others – Apple belongs here as well – have understood at the deepest level that to make accessible – we could say, to commoditize – experiences that are normally available to a tiny elite of highly trained athletes and artists, to introduce the man and woman in the street, even fleetingly, to what it feels like to stretch our capabilities to the limit, is to create personal and brand meaning of the most desirable and memorable form.

This, we could say, is the stuff of dreams. And the few

brands that reach this level are rewarded with unprecedented customer attention, spend, loyalty and advocacy.

Everywhere at once

Zygmunt Bauman and Douglas Rushkoff, who enter the discourse from quite different trajectories, have important and challenging points to make about the human condition when thrown onto The Network.

In their recent work, both address the abrupt dislocations and reversals that are consequences of this shift.

Bauman, in many senses taking the work of Anthony Giddens forward (where Giddens writes of 'late modernity', he dives right in and calls it 'liquid modernity'), stresses the endless flow of liquid life, and its contrast to the relative solidity, security and also morality of the past.

The book that gives the most accessible introduction to and summary of Bauman's work is *Liquid Times*, a dense but wide-ranging explanation of his concerns.

Social institutions are significantly diluted. He describes a 'network nomadism', where, in return for an apparently unbounded freedom of choice and movement on The Network, people sacrifice – consciously or otherwise –

feelings of consistent identity, belonging and sustainable, shared meaning.

The overriding picture here is a paradoxical one of hyper-connected isolation. It's therefore hard to shake off the dystopian implications of Bauman's work. Not that his approach is in any way cold or lacking in compassion: he is insistent on looking for the positive in the future.

Rushkoff, while landing in a field not far from Bauman's, has come into the debate from a previous career as an electronic artist and cyber-theorist. As such, his earlier output tended towards a digital utopianism, which has tempered over time, to now provide still startling but well-balanced insights into humanity on The Network.

If Bauman picks up from Giddens, Rushkoff has consistently drawn heavily on the thinking of McLuhan. As a result, he is in terms of both core stance and references very much a media theorist.

His most recent book, *Present Shock* (referring back to, while also radically updating, Toffler's *Future Shock*) lays out an argument rich in astringent observations. Two, in terms of our concerns here, bear a closer look.

Rushkoff writes (and also speaks, by the way, with charm and persuasion) about the collapse of everything into the here and now.

The Network presents us with ever-greater amounts of stimulation that finds us wherever and whenever we are. We wait, in fact, for almost nothing anymore: so much of our world comes to us.

Rushkoff takes this point to a further level with his concept of 'narrative collapse', the end of meaningful story as a staple of culture, marketing and communications.

His point, if we accept it, has profound implications that reach right across media to challenge not only long-form content of all kinds, but the future role and value of story in all forms of brand communication.

The rather feeble notion of 'always-on' is abruptly replaced by something far more disruptive: 'everything, always, here and now'.

The co-creation of value

The increasing focus on service and services as sources of new value is familiar to all of us. The digital revolution and the disruptive effect of The Network clearly both accentuate and accelerate the importance of a service-based philosophy.

However the foundations and implications of this way of thinking have not generally been sufficiently examined, not least because they are in themselves extremely disruptive.

Two academics who have made this their own exclusive project are Robert Lusch and Stephen Vargo, whose work on Service-Dominant Logic (SDL) is central to understanding the underlying changes in the nature of value, its creation, distribution and exploitation.

Lusch and Vargo have been publishing the results of their work for over two decades, and the significant chasm between its broad and enthusiastic uptake in academic circles, and its lack of penetration into commercial insight and strategy speaks volumes of just how challenging their approach is to the status quo.

Readers will need to familiarize themselves with the work itself – an ideal starting point is their recent book, *Service-Dominant Logic – Premises, Perspectives and Possibilities*.

Alongside the evident resistance to their radical and – be assured – crucial contribution to the litany of cutting edge insight for strategy, we should note that while they, to date, have stopped short of prescribing a methodology for the enterprise adoption of SDL, the precision and simplicity of their overall argument makes it an essential preparation for doing business on The Network.

The core principles of SDL are both startling and familiar. Quoting directly from the book itself, we can see just how profound their rethink of traditional market structures is:

- Service is the fundamental basis of exchange;

- The customer is always a co-creator of value;

- All economic and social actors are resource integrators;

- Value is always uniquely and phenomenologically determined by the beneficiary.

Mapping SDL onto our own argument, the implications are deeply challenging but also exciting. We see the beginnings of a fresh rationale for value that feels, once we get over the shock, both robust and reassuring.

Above all, the increasing dissolution of the traditional breach between enterprise and customer – we build this, they consume it, and never the two shall meet – is given a logic and a shape that prepares us to radically rethink how we relate to customers who are becoming, if anything, as active and influential on The Network as any enterprise.

Chapter summary

- The most important lessons about customers on The Network emerge from the cultural and social theory of the past 60 years;

- Media technologies systematically shift power to individuals and their tribes;

- The management of personal identity, social belonging and shared meaning have been revolutionized by the move to The Network;

- Connected individuals now represent a powerful 'Fifth Estate' that can organize around shared values and concerns;

- Human experiences and expectations are transformed and elevated by The Network;

- When everything converges around the individual at the same time and place, the traditional role played by narrative – the value of stories – is removed, with significant consequences for brands and media owners;

- The previously sharp distinction between enterprise, brand and customer dissolves, as each becomes a co-creator of value on The Network.

Liquid customers

9

The challenge of finding common ground on The Network • changes in the nature and location of trust • understanding service value • experience and expectation.

From culture to customer

I've touched very lightly – without doing any of them justice – on a tiny selection of the work of a small group of thinkers who I believe, precisely because they rarely focus on business strategy or marketing theory and practice (Service-Dominant Logic being the exception), are able to help us begin to make sense of human experience on The Network.

Never more so than today, we need to learn to view our customers through their own side of the looking glass.

We can then, albeit imperfectly, begin to extract from

the fragments of social, cultural and media theory presented above, what it might mean to be a customer on The
Network.

The fragmentation of meaning

Threaded through the work of every major commenta-
tor here is the profound shift in how meaning is created,
shared and received on The Network.

It's no surprise that traditional institutions – in particular
the nation state – wield far less influence than in pre-connected times.

Equally – and the social media explosion of the past
decade is naturally a core driver here – the construction
of self-identity that Anthony Giddens documents, fed
through Manuel Castells' global 'networks of power and
outrage' sets the scene for the phenomenon of what we
might call 'the distributed me'.

News, beliefs and commentary from the most trivial
blurt up to profound and important analysis, press in on us
from every direction.

The paradox that this generates, as we see in Zygmunt
Bauman's recent output, combines a sense of unprece-

dented communication power and reach for individual and tribe, with an unmooring from traditions that have previously grounded and contextualized identity, belonging, and of course, meaning.

So the customer on The Network resembles a kind of lonely monarch, with dominion over everything they see, an enormous range of resources – most of them free of charge – at their fingertips, but with a tenuous grasp on what is actually going on, what matters here and now, and what to do about it.

It's well established, for example, that customers pay for this ostensibly cost-free power with significant compromises in privacy. There is, we could say, an ongoing sacrifice here of one kind of self for another. If meaning is, as I believe, best defined in terms of forms and degrees of connection, this customer is both hyper-connected and dislocated.

Taking into account, if we accept his premise, Douglas Rushkoff's point regarding narrative collapse, and bearing in mind that stories, in one form or another, have arguably provided a shared cultural and social foundation that brands have more or less exclusively relied upon for the communication of value, this new fractured fluidity in meaning makes it increasingly challenging to find common ground with customers on The Network.

One thing we can be sure of, just as we've seen how information, far from being a consistent friend to the enterprise, frequently attacks the traditional mechanisms of business, is that the increasingly granular targeting of digital advertising that has featured in the online experience of the past decade is not the answer.

In the absence of any consistent shared context between brand and customer, other sources of connection must urgently be sought.

Trust in tribes

The challenges of customer meaning that now face enterprise and brand both underpin and are echoed by the changes in how trust manifests and is managed on The Network.

Anthony Giddens has written extensively on how risk, in a cultural and social context that is itself so fluid and fast-moving, from being formerly an occasional concern triggered by specific external events, is now sensed as a constant undercurrent in the individual's daily life. The implications for trust are significant.

Like meaning, trust is a multi-faceted concept that defies easy definition. But just as I like to frame meaning in the basic terms of connection, I find it pragmatic to approach trust as 'the thing that enables us to move forward with relative ease in the face of a degree of uncertainty'.

We see immediately that, one way or another, trust makes the commercial world go round.

In the wake of the recent global recession triggered by the credit crunch of 2007, banks and other financial institutions have been troubled by a variety of trust issues.

These do not, as it happens, revolve so much around the old chestnut of secure online payments. Most customers in markets where such services are established are reasonably comfortable with security and, of course, the trade-off in terms of convenience is undeniable.

Banks in particular continue to walk a tightrope between the government bailouts that got them out of jail post-2007, and the apparent need to pay their top performing staff eye-watering bonuses. Given that, for example in the UK, it was the taxpayers themselves who funded the rescues of a number of major banks, this naturally leads to discomfort all round.

But while the banks themselves are, behind the scenes at least, hugely preoccupied with regaining what they see as lost trust, when we look more closely we have to conclude that this is no longer really a matter of trust at all.

There has been no drop in the volume of online transactions by either business or personal banking customers. Apart from exceptional cases, customer trust in terms of security and privacy has not troubled the sector more than we would have expected.

Like any enterprise, major banks are concerned about the perception of their brands by customers. While at a transactional level, beyond regulatory restrictions, there seems to be little to worry about, there's no question that reputations, already fragile before the credit crunch, have been driven brutally further down.

The issue here is not, in fact, about trust as we normally discuss it. Banking's customers, or more specifically, its consumers – since business banking features client relationships that tend to both more hard-edged and more intimate – experience a widening chasm in any sort of shared meaning between themselves, their lives, and the messaging and behaviour of banks.

On one hand, consumer banking's brand communications consistently feature a tone of concerned partnership. 'We've got your back' is the theme. On the other, customers see what typically looks like overtly cynical behaviour among banks.

They just don't like banks or bankers much anymore, and as their previous dependence on these monolithic institutions is diluted by, for example, competition by major retailers for current account, credit card and lending services (often combined with existing loyalty programmes that add further value to the relationship), and disruption by new online and mobile competition that bypasses red tape and streamlines experience by fully leveraging The Network, their reasons to cut the cord are sharpened all the time.

While the kneejerk response of many banks has been to double down on trust, the field of competition here, including the range of available new services with relatively no reputational – or indeed emotional – baggage, is defined by different drivers.

This is a service issue. And as we can see in other sectors, for example marketing and advertising, which are currently undergoing their own Damascene moment as customers – not to mention regulators – push back hard on aggressive tactics of targeting and tracking, the approach that is demanded from here is not built on the management of trust.

It's the effective and transparent balancing of risk and value that holds the key to regaining shared meaning between such brands and their customers. When we are able to harness as much as possible of the potential value that all forms of available data can fuel, to create fresh and meaningful services that, at the same time, manage down risk in a trade-off that is acceptable to customers, we are on the way to renewed opportunity.

Not that trust, as a result, disappears as a fundamental concern for customers. But, as we touched on above, on The Network it is no longer vested in traditional institutions. Rather than looking to enterprises and their brands, we turn, whenever in doubt, to others whose values we more or less share. We go to our various tribes for confirmation and validation.

As trust moves onto The Network, in other words, and assuming that basic transactional security is sustained – now an expected, commodity component of experience – customers are challenging businesses to provide meaningful, distinctive and truly valuable services.

Value in service

The work of Lusch and Vargo on Service-Dominant Logic, while it has yet to land fully in enterprise thinking and strategy, is waiting in the wings to help transform the way we approach the nature, creation and movement of value on The Network.

In particular, their argument that the division between enterprise and customer is a construct that is of rapidly diminishing usefulness is compelling.

The person formerly known as the customer is not only the final arbiter of value, but is by definition – and this is unquestionably so given the dynamics of The Network, and the service-based models that enterprise offerings are obliged to adopt – invariably involved to a greater or lesser degree as a co-creator of that value with the brand.

What is the potential role of the enterprise here?

There are three forms of service value we can offer to customers, once we come to see the new shape of the opportunity.

First, we can extend what brands have always done as advertisers, which is to embed a message in some form of entertainment. When applied to an intelligent contextual service, we describe this as enhanced service. Of course, it only makes sense to enhance something that the customer finds enjoyable.

Second, shifting the focus of value from entertainment towards utility, we can reduce complexity and legwork in a customer's execution of a purpose or a smaller task. Let's call this streamlined service.

Third, pushing deeper into utility, we can remove work (and in certain instances, risk) for the consumer altogether.

Automated services of this kind tend also to become 'invisible': given the emerging embedded intelligence that we can expect from the IoT, it's these automated forms of customer value that are both the most exciting and the most disruptive, and naturally enough, also the hardest to discover.

Experience and expectation

Where brands in the world of the pre-connected customer were largely built on the model we discussed earlier – the promise of the communication, followed and tested at some later point by the delivery of value in the experience of ownership in some form – on The Network, customers continuously encounter and assess brands in a fluid model that permits no long-term assumptions by the enterprise.

Amidst the turbulence that defines the environment, a new, live and constantly shifting dynamic emerges, which takes the form of an ongoing cycle of experience and expectation.

Customers experience a piece of the brand in the form of a service encounter. They may bring vague or precise preconceptions to the encounter, but these will be less shaped by the previous communications of the brand itself and far more by, for example, tribal messaging that derives from the experiences to date of other customers to whom this individual is connected on The Network.

The immediate experience and its quality create a future expectation, one that frames not only this customer's predisposition when they consider a future re-engagement with the brand, but, in microcosm, the current equity of the brand itself.

Brand equity on The Network therefore becomes, we could say, a fleeting snapshot in time of all the current expectations of every one of its customers, a real time aggregate of a global cloud of both previous and anticipated encounters.

How, therefore, should enterprise leadership both think about and manage brands? What does a brand even mean, and how should it behave on The Network?

Chapter summary

- Finding common ground with a customer whose own identity and sense of meaning are in constant flux is a significant brand challenge that is not met by advertising;

- Dependency on institutional trust is vanishing: for powerful connected customers it is distributed across The Network and framed by delivered value and minimized work and risk;

- Quality and innovation in intelligent services are increasingly meaningful to customers and are informing the growth of the most powerful and competitive brands;

- As such, brand preference and equity are no longer vested in linear promise and delivery, but in an unending, liquid cycle of experience and expectation.

Liquid brands

10

The defensive brand • branding as shared meaning
• customers take control of meaning • brands and
algorithms converge • the new 'network agency'.

A troubled history

Brands have been central to both culture and commerce
for well over a century. It's interesting, in the light of our
argument, to note where they originated.

At the dawn of the seventies Stephen King of J. Wal-
ter Thompson, for many the father of the discipline of
brand planning, published a brief, urgent paper, 'What Is
A Brand?'.

He begins with a direct and passionate challenge to enterprise leadership. His concerns sound remarkably familiar, even close to half a century later:

I wonder whether all top management are involved deeply enough in the nature of their brands. Do they realize fully enough that it is from the success of brands rather than as products that the profits will come? Do they fully understand the nature of brands? Do they set company objectives in terms of brand positioning or simply in financial terms?

The role and value of brands – indeed of marketing as a whole – have struggled mightily for recognition and traction in the boardroom.

Now the unforgiving context within which marketing and advertising must operate has forced branding's confidence and appreciated impact even further into the background.

Given particularly that the balance sheets of many of the world's biggest businesses continue to list brand equity as a dominant line – at the time of writing, for example, the value of the world's most recognized consumer brand, Coca-Cola, is estimated at about $83bn – this is surely a significant concern to enterprise leadership.

King frames branding very much as a defensive imperative, first used by consumer product manufacturers to push back against the wholesalers that dominated consumer product marketing from the late Victorian era, and second – starting in the 1950s – against the retail chains whose dominance of brands' channels to market, along-side their aggressive own-brand programs, created a game of cat and mouse that continues today.

It's worth noting as an aside that, from railways and roads, newspapers and radio, right up to The Network of today, brands have continuously and increasingly been squeezed by networks of one kind or another, as they have evolved over the last century, into defensive positions.

Retailers in particular have continued to challenge man-ufacturers to investigate sources of value, beyond the prod-uct itself, to sustain both preference and margin. The central concept of brand equity is rooted in this requirement.

Mr King completed his paper by pointing to the need for advertising to build and sustain new forms of ownable added value around the consumer brand:

First, we can recognize that in the 1970s it may well have a different role from the past. Added values and their effects on profits will become more important ... Secondly, we can improve our methods of setting ad-vertising's objectives, by thinking of them in terms of the advertising's contribution to the added values of

> *the brand ... And thirdly, we can recognize that ad-*
> *vertising itself is a totality ... If we try to produce it by*
> *the atomistic approach, we will end up with a sort of*
> *Identikit brand ... [which] will never come to life.*

As we read his words, we have feelings of both familiarity and regret. His argument could live very comfortably in any seminar today.

Subsequently, as we explored in Chapter 6, the rapidly growing accessibility and democratization of information has introduced a third player into this sometimes brutal 'Game of Thrones', the increasingly powerful connected customer.

FMCG brands in particular find themselves caught in a pincer movement, with information-powered retailers – on- and offline – ruthlessly pressing down on margins, and consumers able, with little or no effort, to shop for even the most premium brands and secure the lowest possible prices.

If we think of brand equity as netting out in the form of sustainable price levels and consumer preference, both are under systematic attack.

Brand loyalty, itself a central goal of the hundreds of billions of dollars invested annually in advertising – why build a brand that no one comes back to, after all? – is, by extension, consistently undermined.

And of course, intrinsic to this growing challenge is the ever-growing reach and fluidity of The Network.

If this is the current position for brands and branding, historically always troubled, even more so under this constant threat from the erosive impact of retailer and consumer power, what might added value look like, in the context of today's and tomorrow's chronic turbulence?

Marketing for meaning

Behind the received wisdom and standard vocabularies of marketing practice lies a rarely discussed but important constant.

The universal role of branding, before we consider, for example, issues such as brand positioning or its impact on the creating and sustaining of added value, is the development and management of shared meaning between product or service and customer.

The ways in which brands have served to create cultural and social meaning represent in themselves a fascinating story, blending research and creativity to develop some of our most iconic, familiar social touchstones.

Among scores of others, Coca-Cola, Mercedes, IBM and of course Apple – Steve Jobs was an instinctive and sure-footed master of branding – have, alongside their enormous share of market, dominated the world's culture.

They have all, in other words, commanded and exploited the management of meaning.

Broadly, the process has been one of using fresh and profound insights to uncover what we might call 'hidden overlaps' between the customer's everyday life and the purpose and function of the product or service.

Broken connections

Meaning is a rich and complex word. But in the marketing context it boils down to one simple and recognizable fact: it's about a direct, personal connection between brand and customer.

This connection has, until the digital revolution began the still-unfolding process of uncoupling brand from brand communication, been almost entirely driven by advertising.

And it's the ongoing shift, from the messaging of an advertising campaign, via the embedding of meaning in customer-controlled digital experiences – in particular of course social media – to the increasingly hard-fought battle for attention the defines the present and future challenges for brands, that sets the scene for radical transformation in the way brands think about, and can usefully create, meaning.

Meaning has, in the age of The Network, become a key basis of competition, of customer attraction and retention, of advocacy and, as a result, a new paradigm for brand marketing itself.

The strength of a brand is becoming precisely the efficiency and effectiveness with which meaning is created, packaged and delivered, or perhaps more subtly, shared, between business and customer.

This is exactly why brand marketers are so unnerved by the connected consumer. Since the days of the soap opera and its associated soap ads, brands have created meaning for consumers by joining the fragmented media dots: no soap ad, no soap opera.

That's rarely the case now.

When consumers get joined up, they create their own systems of meaning. This is what Facebook has so profoundly understood. It's a factory of meaning, a hive with well over a billion happy worker bees in it.

This, in turn, is why it's regarded with such awe.

Brand as algorithm

Massive varieties and volumes of data flow across The Network. Both are expanding continuously. And while both data and network are crucial to the delivery of value, the creation and development of that value, in the context of transformation, rely almost entirely on the intelligence and adaptability of algorithms.

The enterprises that effortlessly and repeatedly deliver infinite 'Wow!' to their customers are powered by teams of the best engineers in the world.

Their job is to obsessively and ruthlessly build, manage and refine the unique algorithms that will maximize shared meaning between enterprise and customer.

It's worth noting here, if we imagine that we are reaching too far into the intangible future, that Amazon at the time of writing already automatically updates its core algorithms every eleven seconds.

As it happens, brands and algorithms have a lot in common. Among many other functions, both are rules for the creation of meaning.

Now they're coming together to both engineer and communicate entirely new forms of competitive customer value.

If the end role of a brand on The Network is above all to create valued service for customers, the algorithms are becoming more than delivery mechanisms, more than merely the avatar or servant of the brand.

They are, however hard this may be to accept, becoming brands in their own right. They are building customer meaning, trust and value on The Network, in ways we are only just coming to understand.

Network agency

The power and value of a brand, if we accept this argument, cannot be built or measured as before.

The relative success and future prospects of any enterprise on The Network will come to be measured in terms of what we can call 'network agency'.

Visualize network agency as the current and prospective range of the footprint of a brand across The Network.

Into our understanding of this 'agency' we can factor considerations such as the brand's current resilience – its ability to both defend itself and move opportunistically to take advantage of transient opportunities – and also its relative adjacency to such opportunities.

Here our previous brief examination of what we mean by, and how we approach, innovation lands firmly.

A brand's relative agency on The Network provides the ability to go far beyond doing things differently in the hope that speculative investment might be rewarded if things happen to go our way.

It places the brand in adjacent positions to opportunity spaces that can be assessed, planned for and exploited with minimum time and cost and maximum competitive – albeit typically transient – advantage.

This is what we talked about earlier, when we looked at the unprecedented and growing ability of network disruptors to move with ease beyond their sector of origin to capture and dominate others.

Where pre-connected competition dictated that such strategies, mired as they were in traditional assets, capabilities and investment models, would require years of planning, significant cost and high risk of failure, successful competition by brands on The Network will be defined by movements that are decided upon and executed, relatively, overnight.

To perform at this breathtaking level and speed, how will the enterprises that survive and thrive on The Network need to think about and shape themselves, in order to ensure the combination of resilience, agility and sure-footedness that will be required?

Chapter summary

- Since their origins, brands have always been under pressure within their markets, and The Network sharply and continuously increases this effect;

- Their traditional role as bridges of meaning between enterprise and customer must fundamentally evolve in order to retain a viable role on The Network;

- Just as the most successful new enterprises are driven and steered by algorithms that are themselves rules for the creation of meaning, so successful brands will tend to converge with development and management of algorithms, to the point where they will become, for both enterprise and customer, synonymous;

- As a result, brand equity on The Network will come to be managed and measured as 'network agency'.

Liquid enterprise 11

Acceleration, adaptation, automation • letting
go of more old friends • rethinking decisioning,
investment, operations and resource management
• option portfolios as core enterprise assets.

Perpetual transformation

The single lesson that we bring, I hope it's now clear, to examining the new structures and strategies that enterprises wishing to compete on The Network must seek to adopt, is that transformation itself is emerging as their essential core capability.

We talked earlier about the designed disposition of The Network to flow around areas of blockage, to move as fast and as fluidly as possible, and the corresponding risk to enterprises of becoming a sluggish, static, or at worst, 'dead node'.

This risk is real, and if left unaddressed, paralyses the ability of strategy to guide and shape the decisioning and investment required to either defend or grow the business.

In order to align and move with the turbulence of The Network, and also to exert influence on it to grow the brand footprint of network agency, the liquid enterprise must continuously transform to behave in a dynamic, wholly flexible manner that reflects this ultimately inescapable environment.

Before we move on to look at the changes in strategic thinking that will need consideration in the mid- to long-term, there are three simple dimensions of enterprise behaviour that will, from here on, be generic and common leadership imperatives.

These also form a useful lens through which to assess, evaluate and measure our ongoing investments in the intrinsically necessary 'rolling tactics' we looked at early in the book: digital business transformation, customer experience, and innovation.

At its heart, the perpetually transforming liquid enterprise must constantly evolve to become quicker, more adaptable, and able to more or less continuously automate as many of its functions, systems and processes as possible.

We can call these basic dimensions of change the three 'A's.

Acceleration

When we agonize about disruption, our fundamental issue, whether declared or otherwise, is clock speed.

The market, the competition, and perhaps above all, the customer, all seem constantly to be accelerating away from us.

The familiar reference points for disruption, Uber, Airbnb and their peers, are 'pure network' players whose explosive growth, remarkable valuations and destructive impact on incumbents are propelled not by internal enterprise agility – though that is of course important – but by their ability to exploit the external acceleration of network value.

These well-known brands notwithstanding, the stark disparity between corporate and market clock speed places a challenge that, even considered in isolation, can feel impossible to meet.

Adaptation

Perhaps the best work on the endgame for enterprise certainty is Rita McGrath's recent book, *The End of Competitive Advantage.* While the introductory sections are concerned with the reasons for, and consequences of, the headline challenge, the work really takes hold when McGrath introduces and articulates her core concept of 'transient competitive advantage'.

This, of course, is all about adaptability, the ability to alter strategy and implement at speed, in response to relevant changes in opportunity. And here we mean anticipated opportunity, not just what's happened in the past.

Where we have traditionally, and often successfully until recently, developed a new product or service and taken it to the market, from a strategic angle the growing need, we could say, is to take 'the market to the product', shifting the focus outside the enterprise to appreciate and grasp the latent value that The Network offers.

Automation

In lock-step with Acceleration and Adaptation, our third challenge demands that we consistently look to transition

– and having done that, continually further optimize and streamline – as many key processes as we can to become automated and, equally critical, integrated systems.

Everything that can become software, must become software.

One of the more sobering realizations is that human processes, in areas where information technology can usefully and economically both replace and transform them, pose a direct threat to efficiency.

This sounds – and indeed is – a grim consideration with an immense range of consequences for human work, life and, in extreme cases, survival. The hope is that the automation we'll increasingly see implemented will in turn realize new forms of value-added work to replace the eventually redundant tasks.

For now, we must put these important moral questions to one side.

The fact is that Automation is, for both upstart and incumbent, an entirely necessary and central concern and focus.

Letting go of more old friends

While the three 'A's are in some ways a reassuring – by dint of at least being familiar – set of dynamics that we can more or less envisage in terms of our experience to date, they are not in isolation sufficiently transformative to provide the enterprise with the future liquidity that The Network demands.

Here, two deeply entrenched and long-trusted touchstones, assumptions that have stood us in excellent stead until now, need to be let go.

The core mental model that underpins and informs the strategy, planning, briefing and management of the majority of pre-connected enterprises assumes:

- First of all that linear, rigid projects or programmes are the essential instruments of efficient and effective change.

- Second, once this change is achieved, the key processes and dynamics both within and between the affected operating areas will remain more or less fixed and fit for purpose.

Two central limitations in the enterprise operating model result from these philosophies:

- The organization remains too rigid to adjust internally: while the components of the business may be improved, their dynamics are not.

- External changes are experienced as negative, surprise disruptions, rather than anticipated and potentially advantageous competitive opportunities.

Before moving on, a residual point needs to be made in terms of project delivery success rates.

While it's already painfully understood that in the region of 70% of enterprise projects are considered more or less outright failures, even the present day complexity of the environment, if we were to assume that levels of turbulence were to remain static, dictates that it is now effectively impossible for a significant project to be delivered against the original requirement.

The Network, to reiterate, has already eroded much of the desired certainty of execution that has informed our strategies and plans to date.

How then, must we rethink the way we think, in order to support the evolution of the liquid enterprise? How, tangibly, does perpetual transformation manifest in the management of the key levers of a business?

Managing decisions

We talked right at the beginning of the book about the role of enterprise leadership revolving largely around the management of certainty.

Decisions have traditionally been, first of all, based on the careful sifting and consideration of all available and relevant evidence, and second, a commitment to a more or less binary, yes or no, decision to invest in a project or a series of projects that are intended, over time, to meet the overall enterprise priorities and specific strategic objectives at the time of decision.

I hope we now understand the landscape and implications of The Network sufficiently to see that will we no longer have the luxury of such relative simplicity.

Management decisioning – and indeed this philosophy must cascade across all key enterprise disciplines – will need to shift radically from the previous binary, yes or no model, with a primary dependence on evidence, and a secondary one on confidence, informed, in particular, by past and present leadership experience, expertise and profile.

The new model will depend primarily on ever-changing degrees of relative confidence, informed far less by leadership's past history and credibility, and far more by a continuous, present and future-focused view of relevant activity and potential value and risk implications on The Network, with an important but secondary dependence on evidence.

To make appropriate, viable decisions in the turbulent context of The Network, leadership decisions therefore shift from conclusive commitments that launch long-term, fixed projects, to incremental, confidence-focused commitments that optimize value and risk by assessing and selecting from a wide variety of options.

Key yes or no decision points are replaced by changing degrees of certainty, expressed as incremental decision thresholds that trigger equally gradual, conditional management and implementation responses.

The implications of this profound change point to a concern that has been bubbling away for a while in advanced project management circles: is the project, as a vehicle for enterprise change and growth, nearing the end of its days?

Managing investment

Investment models have to date been broadly focused on commitment to the acquisition – either by direct ownership or other means – of assets that are seen as critical to enterprise growth.

The recent and increasing parallel movements of core business processes to outsourcing, and core technologies to the cloud, can be seen as early pointers in the direction of a far more flexible approach, which, by extension, will prepare us for effective competition on The Network.

However, a further shift is now demanded, one where our estimation of the relative value and risk associated with not just the ownership and internal management of such assets, but their very tendency to trap the enterprise in processes and capabilities that may be fit for purpose now, but are sure to encounter challenges soon enough, needs serious revision.

Just as we have seen with the move away from binary to incremental management decisioning, increasing omni-directional turbulence makes all fixed commitments to assets, whatever the model of access and ownership may be, into potential future threats.

Where, up to now, capital assets have typically played a very positive part on the balance sheet, they will come to be seen, and eventually evaluated, as potential liabilities.

Our focus therefore needs to move to a new kind of asset, one where investments in latent, in-waiting skills and capabilities are consistently assessed, re-evaluated in full context, and triggered by the decision thresholds mentioned above.

In sharp contrast to the capital asset model of valuation, it is the relative resilience of our portfolio of strategic and tactical options, whose interdependency is actively tracked from out on The Network, to inside and right across the liquid enterprise, that will determine the robustness, present value and future promise of the business.

Managing operations

From management of decisions and investment, we move logically to look at operational management.

Again, the mental shift is a big one. As a useful analogy, you'll remember we looked early in our story at how Google's revolutionary PageRank changed the way the Web was searched.

Where previously the entire emphasis of the industry had been on indexing the contents of webpages themselves, Page and Brin realized that it was the dynamics that clustered and evolved around the pages, the associated trails of user behaviour on The Network, that determined both far more accurately and, importantly, fluidly over time, the match between search and results.

In a similar way, and informed by the same premises as the changes required in decisioning and investment, enterprise operations will need to move their long-established primary attention from managing processes within divisions of the business, to managing – with what today may seem like unachievable agility of response to changes on The Network – dependencies between, as well as within, these divisions and their processes.

In the absence of our making this challenging and counter-intuitive journey through the looking glass, to manage what may feel like intangible, ethereal entities, our operations become decreasingly responsive to a market context that simply moves at an entirely different pace and rhythm. We are, in other words, in danger of becoming dead nodes on The Network.

Managing resources

The sequence in which we have looked so far at the previous enterprise implications culminates in how we will need to correspondingly manage the allocation of resources.

Clearly a straight line model, based on the hitherto accepted approach of the fixed project, comes increasingly into question, as The Network exerts its growing pressure on the assumptions that have informed the specification of the required work at its inception.

As we've discussed more than once, today the chances of successful delivery are already far too slight for comfort. Contrasting the hard-wired, time- and cost-based management of most current projects, with the turbulent context that will be pulling against them from all directions even before development begins, we're forced to consider alternative strategies for resource allocation.

The problem, we come to realize, is that this turbulence continuously impacts and changes both the nature and location of value itself as such projects roll on. And they are not typically equipped – either philosophically or practically – to adjust their delivery programmes, when the intended deliverables themselves are thrown into such doubt.

So it's the ability of an enterprise to adjust its response to these capricious shifts in value – changes in opportunity and threat, we can also call them – that needs our attention.

Again, our earlier point about focusing on the active management of dynamics comes into play, challenging us to unpick the hard-wiring of the current project model, and equipping management to uncouple itself from the fixed imperatives of the original specification, to reshape the work as directly as possible in response to how in-market value itself changes over time.

The corresponding deliverables as a result shift from project outputs, to value-based outcomes that, from the start and throughout, must be treated as variable.

The key resources for delivery are the competencies of individuals, or small teams. Just as cash and time need to be devoted to what is most valuable now, so do competencies.

Using options permits greater liquidity of competence. Skills can be moved to where they add most value.

Critical specialisms that are only infrequently needed can be hired from one of the growing number or organizations that are emerging to manage dynamic supply.

The allocation of resource, when we eventually learn to

get this right, thus moves ever closer to the creation of current, fresh and relevant value on The Network.

This consequence is naturally hard to accept, until we have fully internalized the idea of the end of sustainable competitive advantage, and transferred our allegiance onto a far more opportunistic model, one where we aim to seize transient advantage when and where we are able, and equally to detach and realign as soon as the market shifts and value fades away again to land, more or less temporarily, elsewhere.

Chapter summary

- Perpetual transformation is emerging at the core enterprise capability for survival and success on The Network;

- Threaded across all activities will be the generic imperatives of Acceleration, Adaptation and Automation;

- Long-held assumptions regarding the role of projects, and the rigid shape of the enterprise, will need to be let go;

- Management decisions will be rooted less in evidence and more in the active management of confidence;

- The primary vehicles of change will no longer be large, discrete projects, but extensive and flexible portfolios of options, which will be assessed and triggered incrementally, according to thresholds of confidence;

- Investment will no longer be focused on fixed assets, but on this fluid and constantly updated range of options;

- Operational focus will shift from managing processes within rigidly connected divisions of the enterprise, to highly flexible dependencies between and within these divisions, which are informed and impacted by the movements of value and risk on The Network;

- Resource management will move away from delivering the outputs of fixed projects to managing – by drawing on the enterprise's flexible portfolio of options – highly variable and value-based outcomes.

Liquid leadership

12

The changing demands on leadership • journeys
that had endings • leadership as guardians of
enterprise purpose • lessons from the All Blacks •
how enterprise purpose ensures enduring shared
meaning with customers.

In the eye of the storm

We conclude by looking at some of the key personal and
professional implications for leadership of the enterprise in
a future context defined by chronic turbulence.

Much continues to be written in the field of leadership,
and much of what is written, in particular regarding generic
approaches and techniques, is likely to be of some use in
the future.

However, given the types of extraordinary changes we
are beginning to see, their growing impact on leadership,

and especially the dominant themes of not only grasping chronic uncertainty, but the imperative of converting it to competitive advantage, it's important to consider at least the broadest potential changes in the shape of this crucial role.

What are the expected functions and impacts of a leader in these circumstances?

What does he or she stand for?

Indeed, where to stand at all, when both The Network and the enterprise are engaged in what will be experienced as a rapid, complex and unpredictable dance?

We have come to see that the development of radically different management philosophies and business capabilities is required of the liquid enterprise. Their effective evolution and delivery over time require in themselves a revolution in strategic thought and application.

In particular, as we discussed in the previous chapter, the shift of focus from the linear planning and execution of discrete, more or less divisionally based projects – a series of fixed transformations, we could say, after which business returns to some sort of predictable normality – to an options-based model where the changing shape of value and opportunity on The Network is reflected and, wherever possible, turned into transient advantage, demands that perpetual transformation itself become the core capability of any credibly defensible business.

When understood and converted into a fundamentally new shape for enterprise strategy and operations, uncertainty itself, as was proposed at the beginning of the book, thereby becomes the field of competition.

On the one hand, this logic that informs the evolution of the liquid enterprise is reassuring – we are provided with a contextual framework enabling the interpretation of, and reaction to, turbulent change.

On the other, there is a further transformation that is demanded. Leadership itself, already under unprecedented pressure to define and deliver tangible, sustainable business results in a context that openly defies the techniques and cases that have guided us in the re-connected age, must consider and commit to a corresponding set of quite different roles and responsibilities.

With The Network spinning around the enterprise, and the enterprise itself spinning in response and exerting influence – in the form of network agency – wherever it can, can leadership somehow hold a meaningful position in the eye of the storm?

The answer, of course, is that it must.

But as the traditional function, where the top team in an enterprise sets a course, fixes the tiller, observes and reports back to stakeholders as a series of linear projects unfolds to deliver against the envisioned long-term goals, fades, to be replaced by an aggressive liquidity defined largely by the active management of confidence in response to weather that will never entirely settle, a range of personal and professional challenges emerges.

The hero's journey?

In the eye of any storm, it's crucial to find and hold onto something that is, if not exactly fixed, then solid and consistent enough to provide a degree of security. This is surely a significant part of leadership's future role, and of course, in principle it's not an unfamiliar one.

Books on leadership are full of inspiring stories of iconic men and women who have steered businesses through odysseys of profound threat and emerged triumphant. The stories of those who didn't make it are understandably lower in profile.

Rightly energizing and reassuring as these narratives

are, they do not prepare us for the leadership of the liquid enterprise. The conclusive navigation of a crisis in business, and of course the framing of the journey as a story, are both underpinned by the expectation of an eventual return to business as usual.

In other words, a homecoming to at least relative certainty.

This underlying assumption, as we've explored here, is no longer valid.

It's worth noting as a pertinent aside that, for the first time in history, the consensus, as we gingerly emerge from the global economic crisis that arrived in 2007, is that there will be no going back to the way things were. The shattered confidence, both of and in the financial markets, has left fault lines deep in the foundations of global business.

When conditions are unlikely, in the foreseeable future at least, to return to anything resembling calm predictability, and to the contrary, the chronic and increasing turbulence of The Network provides an inescapable context for competition, the roles of a leader as, for example, either the explosive iconic hero who saves the day, or alternatively the wise, steady hand at the tiller of the enterprise, are pushed into the past.

The core of purpose

At the heart of the liquid enterprise, as the constantly moving parts inside the business, and the chaotic flux of The Network that flows through and around it, continue to change position and shape, lies the one thing that needs to remain consistent.

It's the purpose.

Purpose here means a reason for being, a reflection of the core value to customers that the business stands for, and a touchstone of strategic navigation.

Purpose is where, in the end, every major decision, every critical commitment that the business makes, must land.

In the more forgiving pre-connected era, a lack of clear, consistent, well-articulated and managed purpose, or alternatively its being mistaken for 'what we do', 'the products or services we produce', and often, of course, the brands that represent the business, has not intrinsically threatened its well-being or indeed its survival.

But when everything inside and outside the business is in turbulence, it's our purpose that determines how and why we make decisions and commitments, and how we interpret and reinterpret what is right in terms of value and growth.

Purpose, in fact, becomes the rock of ongoing certainty and shared meaning upon which the liquid enterprise either stands or falls.

Winning with purpose

Just like military history, sport has long been a happy hunting ground for leadership and for business strategy.

There is perhaps, in this case, no sport that is closer to the dynamic and tone of the turbulent, sometimes violent, field on which the liquid enterprise must learn to operate, than rugby.

The most successful rugby team in the world, indeed the most successful international sports team in history, is New Zealand's All Blacks.

Their winning record speaks for itself. Their physical and mental toughness are legendary. Their skill, discipline, speed of play and sheer flair are breath-taking.

Looking back to the previous chapter, and the critical role of managing a portfolio of options, the All Blacks are established masters of this capability.

The team and its management, especially in the wake of a painful series of disappointments in five World Cups – by the time they reclaimed the title, having won the inaugural championship at home in 1987, it was 2011 – has consistently turned to its heritage, its culture, and its purpose to awaken, to drive and guide its attitude and behaviour.

Every All Black, irrespective of impact on the field, seniority or public profile, takes his turn to sweep the changing room after practice. This in itself tells us much of what we need to know about the culture.

Time spent training mind and body are carefully balanced. The intelligence and experience of the coaching staff, and the relentless drills that make every variety of set play automatic on the day, go without saying. No team is better prepared for contingencies.

And on match day, its ability to both adjust and raise its game according to weather conditions, the strategy and tactics of opponents, and, most important in this context, the unexpected threats and opportunities that the nature of this tough, highly cerebral game throws into play is where all this work lands, to make the All Blacks undisputed world champions, as well as the greatest ambassadors of the game.

'Great people make great All Blacks'

However, it's the off-the-field culture, the sense of heritage, the balance of honour and humility – in itself a manifestation of the traditional and powerful Maori value of 'mana' – that inform the extraordinarily effective machine that is the All Blacks' indomitable purpose.

In his very useful book, *Legacy*, James Kerr has explored the lessons that this remarkable institution holds for leadership in both personal and professional life. The work is full of anecdotes, and interviews with legendary players, but most importantly, it asks direct questions about the qualities that propel the All Blacks to success year after year.

For many fans of the sport, Ritchie McCaw is the greatest All Black in history. He is, at the time of writing, about to retire after playing over 140 games in the black shirt, having led the team – and, given its unbridled passion for the sport and the team, the entire New Zealand nation – to victory in two consecutive World Cups.

McCaw is a leader in an organization full of natural leaders. His abilities as a player of the game, as one of the world's top flankers, are a given.

Whether diving into rucks to magically turn over the ball

and claw the fortunes of the game back to the All Blacks, making on the spot tactical calls, or with equal grace accepting victory or defeat, Ritchie McCaw embodies in every aspect of his deportment, the leadership qualities that we can most aspire to in leading the liquid enterprise.

When the All Blacks come to replace him, as they must, they will of course be seeking one of the best players of the sport.

But they will, above and before anything else, select an individual who, as McCaw has unflaggingly done over a long career at the top of the top rugby team in the world, represents and enacts the purpose of the All Blacks.

In the end, it's all about the purpose. This single imperative is the beating heart of the future role of leadership.

Building meaning with the customer

A significant element of purpose is, naturally, a sense of meaning. We've returned to meaning repeatedly in recent chapters, understanding it as an increasingly central currency of the value that is shared between brand and customer.

Just as we've talked about the threat of becoming a dead node on The Network through failure to adapt to its increasing velocity and complexity, a failure to actively manage enterprise purpose at the very heart of the business will lead, soon enough, to a collapse of shared meaning with our customer.

Even more than the co-creation of value on The Network that we touched on previously, the co-creation of meaning is utterly fundamental to sustaining the health and future viability of the enterprise.

With a consistent core thread of meaning running through all the different strategies, tactics, products and services that we bring to bear on the immense challenge of repeatedly finding and exploiting value in chronic turbulence, there is a belief that is shared across brand and customer, a solid reference point that never needs to waver, and an associated set of core values that bind the members of the liquid enterprise together, and in turn, the enterprise to its customers.

So perhaps paradoxically, the future role of leadership will at the broadest level be a combination of cheerleader for the ongoing coherence and morale of colleagues, staff and partner businesses who, while not living and working in the eye of the storm, will be directly and inescapably affected by it in unprecedented ways, and steward of a continuing, highly flexible and yet cohesive connection with customers on The Network.

The personal and professional impacts of such responsibilities will demand more, and also far more diverse forms of, skill, resilience, and above all, focused creativity from leadership than is currently taught anywhere in the world.

To live and come to terms with the conflicting forces that are coming to bear, to take on and deliver an entirely new strategic and operational shape to the enterprise, and from there to sustain a robust sense of meaningful purpose, while everything around us, except that purpose, is in flux, are challenges that few individuals, if they're honest, would relish.

Leading the liquid enterprise will perhaps be the hardest, and therefore, for at least a small group of courageous candidates, the most satisfying job on the planet.

Chapter summary

- The future of business on The Network requires a profound rethink not just of the structure and behaviour of the enterprise, but of the nature and impacts of leadership;

- The shift to uncertainty as the key source of competitive advantage demands of leadership an unprecedented blend of character, flexibility and resilience;

- At the very heart of the role lies the stewardship of the purpose of the liquid enterprise;

- In terms of winning with purpose, the All Blacks, the most successful team in international sporting history, have important lessons for us;

- As well as guiding the liquid enterprise though the turbulent storm of business on The Network, the correct and consistent stewardship of purpose will ensure that a powerful thread of meaning is actively sustained and shared between brands and customers;

- Leading the liquid enterprise will be the most demanding, and therefore valued, role in the future of business on The Network.

Thirteen things

13

Before we part company, here are some final suggestions to both frame the discussion so far, and help you crystallize what I hope has been a useful process that begins to change the way we think about the future of the enterprise.

Each recommendation references a key stage in the narrative so far.

As I suggested in the introduction, please also email me with your observations, builds and challenges. Nothing here is remotely sacred.

1. In the context of chronic turbulence, think about uncertainty as both a dominant feature of the competitive environment, and a new source of competitive advantage for the enterprise.

2. Be wary of viewing your responses to disruption exclusively through a lens of technological innovation, on

the assumption that this, alongside access to the right sources of data, will replace the certainty that the dynamics of The Network have removed.

3. Be equally wary of envisioning customer experience as a series of point solutions that are locked into your sector and brand; actively seek the integration opportunities that reach beyond these into related sectors, to capture a greater share of relevant and differentiated customer service value.

4. Try to become comfortable with the changes in brand building that The Network is driving across many sectors, moving away from messaging and towards intelligent service value.

5. Don't approach innovation as something that 'just needs to happen' and is driven by external stimuli – for example focusing exclusively on relationships with start-ups; try to actively align and manage it with future customer and enterprise value on The Network.

6. Move on from seeing value as primarily created within the enterprise, to be distributed to the market via familiar channels; see it as evolving to become a wide

variety of latent opportunities that are already being created by activity on The Network, to be harvested by the fastest-moving and most adaptable competitors.

7. If your business is located in a previously stable sector-based value chain that is susceptible to disruption by The Network, begin to think about operating in one or more of the developing ecosystems that will extend beyond current industry sectors, to offer new forms of customer value.

8. Keep track of whether your business stands to gain, lose, or both, from the increasing penetration of the Internet of Things into susceptible areas such as transport, logistics, security, product packaging and customer services.

9. Get used to the idea of customers as powerful actors on The Network, whose experiences, expectations and increasing co-creation of value will directly and unpredictably drive shifts in both opportunity and threat.

10. Actively focus on value, no longer as merely embedded in a fixed product or service, but now determined by the customer, and experienced as a highly flexible

currency in the holistic and fast-moving context of The Network.

11. Make the leap to understanding the convergence on The Network of brands and algorithms, to create active, intelligent vehicles for distinct and meaningful services that can compete both within and across sectors.

12. Think about engineering future enterprise change no longer by using fixed and linear projects, but by leveraging a changing portfolio of options, to make transformation itself the new core capability of the enterprise.

13. Finally, try to get comfortable with the stewardship of purpose as a central role for leadership, in order to sustain meaning, both inside and around the enterprise, when the turbulence of The Network consistently challenges its value and its shape.